Decorating

with

Jane Churchill

and

Annie Charlton

Decorating

with
Jane Churchill
and
Annie Charlton

❖

Harry N. Abrams, Inc.

Publishers

Library of Congress Cataloging-in-Publication Data
Churchill, Jane.
[Decorating ideas]
Decorating with Jane Churchill and Annie Charlton : distinctive
ideas for your home from two of Britain's most popular decorators / by Jane Churchill and Annie Charlton.
p.   cm.
Originally published: Decorating ideas. HarperCollins Publishers,
1994
Includes bibliographical references.
ISBN 0–8109–3231–8 (HC)
1. Interior decoration—Handbooks, manuals, etc.   I.   Charlton,
Annie.   II. Title.
NK2115.C49   1996
747—dc20   95–34372
                                                CIP

Text and illustrations copyright © 1994 HarperCollins
First published in 1994 in the United Kingdom by HarperCollins Publishers, London,
under the title *Decorating Ideas*. Created for HarperCollins by Amazon Publishing, Ltd.
Published in 1996 by Harry N. Abrams, Incorporated, New York
A Times Mirror Company
No part of the contents of this book may be reproduced without the written permission
of the publisher
Printed and bound in Italy
The publishers would like to thank Jennifer Jones and Helen Dickenson, who wrote the
introductions

96- 995

Contents

Introduction

There is something particularly satisfying about transforming the appearance of a room with clever decorative techniques. Whether you apply special paint effects to walls or furniture, stencil your own designs, make imaginative use of materials or add decoration to turn an everyday object into something quite stunning, the end result is bound to be rewarding because you will have created, in however small a way, your own personal decorating 'look'.

With over twenty five years of interior decorating experience behind us, we have designed rooms of every imaginable shape, size and style. In all cases the key to success lies in the mixing of colours, patterns, textures and decorative objects to create an attractive overall effect which both reflects the owners' tastes and is individual.

Individuality is a very important element in the look of a room, and often comes from the finishing touches - the detailed features which bring out its style and add character. They can be anything from furniture transformed with tartan to decoratively disguised baked beans cans; or from shelled mirrors to painted sisal mats.

While hunting for places where we could buy decorative items, we discovered dozens of artists and craftsmen, operating from small workshops all over the country, who specialise in making beautiful objects using the traditional methods. So impressed were we by their talent and what they produced that we went on to make a series of television programmes about them.

It was somewhat frustrating at first, watching these highly skilled people turning out their wonderful results in a way which was beyond our talents. However it gradually dawned on us that with a bit of lateral thinking what looked impossible might actually be quite possible, and we decided to see if we could make the same sort of things, on a much simpler scale, which would create the same sort of effect.

The results of our labours are in this book. Its aim is to encourage anyone who wants to add individual touches to a room by being creative themselves to do so! None of the ideas are expensive, and we have deliberately avoided anything that is too complicated. Apart from the materials all you really need is time, patience and imagination. So be bold - because if we can do it, anyone can!

Jane Churchill

Print Rooms

The print room was a form of interior decoration that was briefly popular in Europe in the late eighteenth century. Prints showing a wide range of subjects – from classical scenes to reproductions of popular contemporary paintings – were all the rage at this time. In fact, such was the demand that print makers would even hire out the most recently produced prints for the evening. Usually, the prints were pasted directly onto the wall and were grouped together in symmetrical arrangements. Religious subjects, pastoral scenes, contemporary portraits and classical figures were all displayed together. Each print was framed with a paper border, and decorative elements were added, such as paper *trompe-l'oeil* swags, ropes, chains and cornerpieces.

Since the early 1980s, the print room has gradually come back into fashion in Europe and America. It is a very flexible form of decoration that works just as well in a hallway or stairwell as in a drawing room or bedroom. Reproductions of eighteenth-century prints and print-room decorations are now available from specialist outlets, bringing it within reach of the enthusiastic amateur. However, successfully creating an entire print room requires a good eye and a great deal of patience. For your first project, it is probably a good idea to limit yourself to a small area such as a bathroom or cloakroom. Depending on the availability of prints, you might like to choose a particular theme, one that reflects an interest or hobby. For example, if you are a keen gardener, you could choose prints of flowers and plants, or if you are an angler, you could display fish and fishing scenes. Botanical or architectural prints are particularly satisfying.

Left: Here, a print-room effect works very well on the area of wall above the dado rail.

Before you start work, make sure the surface is matt, or the prints will not stick. A background in earthy colours such as terracotta or yellow ochre looks most attractive with antique prints. Rather than having a flat-painted backgound, you could introduce some texture by sponging or stippling. If you would like your black-and-white prints to look old, soak them briefly in a bath of cold tea (experiment first with a corner of a border for soaking time and depth of colour).

Displaying prints

When it comes to arranging the prints, always start at the centre of the area you are decorating and work your way out. In the eighteenth century, size was more important than subject matter, and the largest print was usually placed in the centre of any grouping. You will need a plumb-line and spirit level in order to establish the true centre – this may seem over-fussy, but it will make all the difference to the finished look. Carefully mark the position of the central print, then start pasting down. If you like, before you stick the prints down permanently, use re-usable adhesive to position them correctly. As you work outwards, it is essential to keep checking that everything is aligned.

In the following project, a small wall area is used to create a simple print room. If you do not want to buy a specialist kit to do this, photocopy prints from magazines and catalogues.

Print Room

You will need:

- Plain, painted wall
- Print-room kit or photocopied prints from magazines and books, and ornamental paper cut-outs and borders available from art and craft shops
- Tape measure
- Spirit level (optional)
- Small pair of scissors
- Re-usable adhesive
- Pencil
- Wallpaper paste
- Paintbrush (to apply paste)

Method

1 If you are not using a print-room kit, choose your prints from magazines, catalogues or books. When photocopying them, make sure you use a high-quality paper. Usual photocopying paper may bubble when the wallpaper paste is applied.

2 Cut out your print borders and any ornamental bits and pieces you want to use. You will need a small pair of scissors, such as nail scissors, to cut out the intricate ornamental pieces (fig A).

3 Mark with a pencil where you want to stick the prints on the wall. To ensure you align the prints correctly, measure the size of each print and then measure in from the corners of the wall. Check with a spirit level, too.

A

B
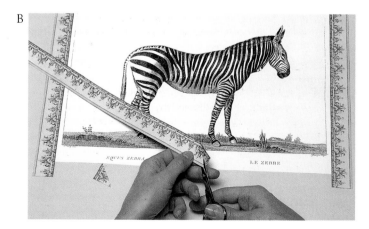

MORE
IDEAS

Use prints and print-room embellishments to decorate other items, such as cabinets, trunks, boxes and screens.

❖

4 Attach the prints with re-usable adhesive. Check they are aligned properly. Once you are happy with the arrangement, glue them on with wallpaper paste.

5 Stick the cut-out borders over the prints. If you are not using a kit, you will have to cut the borders into four pieces and mitre the joints. (A mitred joint is a right-angled corner formed by two strips of material joined together, each having an edge cut at a 45° angle.) To mitre the print borders, fold over the top and bottom of each side border at a 45° angle, then cut off the end **(fig B)**.

6 Place the ornamental bits and pieces around the frame. When you are happy with the effect, paste them on **(fig C)**.

C

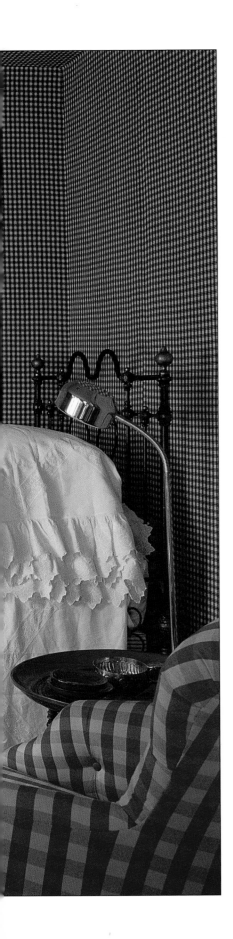

Fabric on Walls

At one time, hanging fabric on walls was as common as painted and wallpapered walls are today. As far back as the ancient Greeks, until the introduction of mass-produced wallpapers in the nineteenth century, hangings provided not only decoration but also a measure of insulation and sound-proofing. As fabric coverings also disguise poor wall surfaces, they were invaluable before the days of the plastered wall.

The simplest way to use fabric is to fix it to the top of the wall and then let it hang down loosely. This was the method favoured by the Greeks and Romans, and their brightly woven or embroidered pieces were supple enough to be gathered and draped around the room and over doorways. In contrast, in the Middle Ages, substantial tapestries were fashionable. Softer hangings of worsted, linen and wool – which were left plain, embroidered or sometimes painted – gradually became more popular, perhaps as much for reasons of comfort as of cost. At the end of the eighteenth century, draping fabric from walls to create a tent-like effect was briefly popular. However, this fashion involved enormous amounts of material, which was very expensive.

In the Middle Ages, wall coverings were hung from rings on a rod or from wooden pegs. This method of displaying fabric works well in most modern interiors, and is a good way to divide up a space – for example, to partition off a sleeping area. Almost any kind of furnishing material can be used hung from a narrow curtain pole fixed to the wall. For a more luxuriant effect, gather a

Left: Use fabric on walls as if it were wallpaper. Here, a checked fabric covers all four walls and the ceiling as well, creating a very cosy effect.

fairly lightweight fabric onto curtain tape and then attach this to a curtain track fixed to a wall.

Working with fabric

Fixing fabric directly to walls first became fashionable in the seventeenth century, and by the eighteenth century it was the most common method used. These days, some fabrics come with a paper backing so that they can be stuck directly to a surface. These include wools, cottons, felts, silks and moirés, and suedes. Wools and silks also come in textured forms; coarser textured wall coverings include hessians, jutes and linens. An alternative is to use ordinary, unpapered fabric, but you will need to screw wooden battens to the wall first to which the fabric can then be secured with nails or staples. If you gather the fabric, each join can be neatly hidden behind the previous pleat. Or make a neat box-pleat as shown in the project that follows. If you are working with a patterned fabric, make sure you match up the pattern. Always finish with a trimming of braid to hide the nails or staples.

Pleated Wallhanging

You will need:

> A piece of fabric the length, and twice the width, of the wall you wish to cover
> Tape measure
> Enough braid to frame the wall area
> Staple gun
> Sewing machine
> Fabric glue

Method

1 Measure the length and width of the wall area you intend to cover.

2 Cut a piece of fabric to the appropriate size (this should be about half of the fabric you have bought). If you have a dado rail, it is better to cover just the area of wall above it. Unless you are confident of your ability, do not choose a patterned fabric such as a check – matching up the squares may cause you problems later on.

3 Staple the fabric you have cut out to the wall at the top and bottom (fig A). You will probably need someone to hold the other end of the fabric as you staple.

4 You need to make 10 cm (4 in) strips to cover the wall, leaving a 10 cm (4 in) gap between each strip. Once you have measured the width of the wall, calculate how many strips you require. To make the strips, cut out double the width of the finished strip. With each strip fold the ends over to make a hem

A

B

C

and machine. Then fold the strip in half, with the wrong side showing. Machine down the edge and then turn the good side out. Once you have made the strip, press the seam so that it lies down the centre back.

5 Leaving 10 cm (4 in) between them, staple on the strips at the top and bottom of the wall (**fig B**). In addition to stapling the strips at the top and bottom, you may need to glue them in the centre to stop them sagging.

6 Measure and cut lengths of braid to run across the top and bottom of the wall area, and two for the sides. Glue the braid over the top, bottom, and side edges of the wall area to cover the staples (**fig C**). Mitre the corners (see page 11).

MORE IDEAS

Calico is a very inexpensive fabric for covering walls. The traditional colour is cream, but some outlets stock calico in a range of colours.

❖

If you have a limited budget, introduce a dado rail (see pages 24–27). Cover the area above the rail with fabric and use paint on the wall below.

Painted Tiles

Decorative wall tiles date back to hundreds of years B.C., when they were first used by the Egyptians to adorn their temples and tombs. Over the centuries, different countries developed their own particular designs, shapes and uses for tiles. In Holland, blue-and-white Delftware tiles were put behind beds, on staircases and around window frames, while in America, large tiles were used in the hallways of grand buildings. Italian craftsmen produced a very different effect by covering their tiles in wonderful transparent glazes. In Victorian Britain, it was fashionable to have individual family portraits painted onto tiles, while in France, seascapes, often in painted in yellow with a blue background, were preferred. As well as being highly decorative, tiles are, of course, eminently practical. As they are easy to clean, adaptable and cool, they are particularly popular in hot counties, especially Spain and Portugal.

For practical purposes, tiles are often used as wall coverings between units in kitchens and bathrooms. When tiling a room, it is not necessary to cover the whole wall area from floor to ceiling. Instead, use just two or three rows of tiles and cover the remaining area with wallpaper or paint. The same tiles can then be used as a border round the mirror, or on top of the surround to a hand basin. An attractive idea for a kitchen wall is to dot single decorated or picture tiles at random among plain ones or to arrange a group of tiles to form a mural. This is particularly effective behind a work surface. White tiles always look smart, especially if you use them with a

Right: A plain white-tiled bathroom is transformed by a scene made up of painted tiles and enhanced by a decorative border.

border of thin rectangular tiles in a strong colour such as dark blue, green or red. You can buy white tiles in slightly larger rectangular shapes. If you arrange these vertically on the wall, they will look very modern. Used cleverly, wall tiles can enhance features in other parts of the house. If you have a wooden staircase you could front the risers with pretty blue-and-white tiles, or you could put them round the inside of a fireplace.

Personalized tiles

You can easily paint plain white tiles yourself, either singly or in a group to form a mural. However, it is important to remember that because they haven't been fired in a kiln, your own painted tiles will not stand up to being scrubbed. Before you begin, they should be cleaned using a damp cloth. If you are not particularly confident about painting, use a stencil or create a simple pattern in spots or stripes, which can then be used as a border. If you intend to paint free-hand, draw the design in pencil before you apply the paint – the pencil markings can be rubbed out when you have finished. A clever idea for a kitchen is to paint individual tiles with objects that you or your family particularly like. This could be anything from a jar of jam to a ladybird. One of the most popular designs for painted tiles is the Delft look, which originated in Holland. In the following project four plain white tiles are painted to form a mural of a blue-and-white jug.

Tile Mural

You will need:

- ➤ Four plain white wall tiles
- ➤ Pretty blue-and-white jug or other piece of china to copy (or a photograph of one)
- ➤ 0.5 lt (1 pt) of warm water
- ➤ Two teaspoons of vinegar
- ➤ Piece of paper as large as the four tiles, divided by pencil lines into four quarters and then into a grid of 2.5 cm (1 in) squares
- ➤ Chinagraph or soft pencil
- ➤ Small jar of dark blue ceramic paint
- ➤ Artist's brush, no 5
- ➤ White spirit to thin the paint
- ➤ Saucer for mixing paint with white spirit

Method

1 On the grid paper, draw the outline of the jug and draw the designs inside the outline. These can be as simple or intricate as you like (fig A).

2 Mix the vinegar and water and use to wash the tiles. Dry the tiles thoroughly.

3 Arrange the tiles in a square on a flat surface. You may need to use double-sided sticky tape underneath to keep them in place while you work on them.

4 With a soft pencil or chinagraph draw the grid and the outline of the jug onto the tiles (fig B).

5 Using the blue ceramic paint and the artist's brush, paint the outline of the jug over the pencil line.

6 Again, using the artist's brush, with the grid drawing as a guide, paint the decoration inside the outline. It is a good idea to paint some of the decoration in a paler blue, which you can achieve by mixing some of the paint with a little white spirit in a saucer (fig C).

7 Leave the tiles to dry for at least a week. Once they are dry, gently rub out any pencil or chinagraph marks that are showing. When attaching these tiles to a wall, it is better to use a tile-fixing adhesive rather than grouting, so that the tiles can be pushed together and the design is kept intact.

A

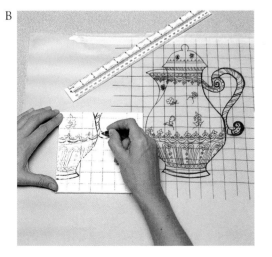

MORE IDEAS

❖

Alphabet tiles are a great idea for your child's room or a bathroom. They are just as educational as blocks, and will not end up littering the floor.

❖

If you are hand-painting plain tiles to use as a border, remember to buy tiles with rounded edges.

Murals

Creating a mural is enormous fun and a great way to allow your artistic side full rein. This does not mean you need the technical and artistic virtuosity of a Michaelangelo – a mural can be as simple as painting a colourful rainbow to frame the door of a child's bedroom, or as small in scale as a trellis covered in climbing plants in an alcove area. Murals do not have to be confined to wall surfaces. Doors and cupboard doors are perfect for this treatment and provide a useful framework within which to work.

The secret to a successful mural is to keep everything simple. Some of the most beautiful and striking examples of murals are the wall-paintings that adorn the tombs of the ancient Egyptians and Etruscans, the palaces of Crete and Roman villas. These murals show stylized images of plants and animals on plain or abstract backgrounds, often with patterned borders. There is always a stunning use of colour.

Whilst these ancient murals provide inspiration, when attempting your first mural you may like to choose a more modern theme. In a child's room, you could paint a blustery sky with clouds and brilliant patches of blue along one or more walls. The sky can then be filled with anything from colourful balloons and kites to your child's favourite fairy-tale or cartoon characters. It is a good idea to paint these separately onto paper or card and stick them onto the wall – this makes them easy to replace as your child's tastes change. In a small dining room or in a corridor, a series of stylized lemon trees in pots (as shown in the following project), perhaps alternating with orange trees, is very attractive. A decorative border above

Left: Murals are effective in almost any room. Here, a mural completes an imaginative bathroom design by adding sails to a ship-shaped bathtub.

and below the trees will clearly define the space. You can either stencil on your border or you can stick down one of the many excellent ready-made border papers that are available.

Creating an illusion

A completely different use of mural-work is *trompe-l'oeil*, the art of tricking the eye. The idea is to create a three-dimensional effect on a flat surface. At its best, it can make you believe, at least for an instant or two, that the image created in paint is real. Although this is probably best left to the professional, if you like this effect there are *trompe-l'oeil* wallpapers available representing, for example, shelves filled with leather-bound and gold-embossed books. You can also try making your own *trompe-l'oeil*, if not on a wall, perhaps on a table, using montage. You can build up a portrait-by-association of a chosen person. For example, if your subject is an enthusiastic card player, stick down some playing cards, the cover of a favourite magazine, and so on. When you have finished, cover everything with a few layers of varnish to seal it.

In the following project, you are shown how to paint a stylized lemon tree. This can stand alone or as part of a frieze.

Lemon Tree Mural

You will need:

- ➤ Plain painted wall or a wall hung with lining paper
- ➤ Pencil
- ➤ Stiff paper or cardboard for stencils
- ➤ Scissors
- ➤ Masking tape
- ➤ Stencil brush
- ➤ Ruler
- ➤ Medium-sized tube of yellow acrylic paint
- ➤ Medium-sized tube of brown acrylic paint
- ➤ Medium-sized tube of green acrylic paint

Method

1 Prepare the wall area. If you are going to paint the mural directly onto the wall, you will need to clean the wall surface first. Or, if you like, you can cover your wall in lining paper, and paint the mural onto this. Obviously the size of the mural depends on the size of the wall. However, you should follow these dimensions: the pot should be smaller than the tree top; the stem should be about three times the height of the tree top. The width of the stem should be about 5–7.5 cm (2–3 in) depending on the size of your tree. Altogether, your mural should be two thirds the height of the wall.

2 Next make the stencils. You will need to make stencils for the lemons, the pot and the leaves. To make your lemon stencils, draw on paper three different sizes of lemons. Then cut out the shapes. If you like, you can copy real lemons. Make the leaf stencils in the same way. An excellent way of drawing the pot outline is to take a sheet of paper and fold it in half. Draw the shape of half a terracotta pot. Cut out the pot shape and open out the paper.

3 Attach your pot stencil to the wall with masking tape. Paint inside the stencil with the yellow acrylic paint. Leave it to dry. Then, with the stencil brush, stipple over the yellow in brown acrylic paint, allowing the yellow to show through **(fig A)**. To stipple, dip the brush lightly in the paint, hold the brush at right angles to the wall and dab the paint on. Do not press too hard.

4 Measure your stem length and width with a ruler and mark it in with pencil.

5 Now, start on the lemon stencils. Hold a stencil against the wall and stipple with the stencil brush using the yellow acrylic paint. Do not put too much paint on the stencil brush as it may drip. If the stencils get a little soggy, let them dry out before you continue.

6 Stick masking tape down the stem outline and with the stencil brush paint with brown acryllic paint. When it is dry (it should only take a few minutes) peel off the masking tape and free-hand, with a small paintbrush, paint in the little stem shoots **(fig B)**.

7 Now turn your attention to the leaves. Using green acrylic paint, stencil them in the same way as the lemons **(fig C)**.

A

B

C

MORE IDEAS

A mural can be created in a variety of mediums. Stencils
(see pages 44–47), rubber stamps or home-made vegetable prints
(see pages 48–51) are all suitable.

❖

A plain door at the end of a long corridor is a perfect site for a mural.

Mouldings

There is so much more you can do to give a stylish finish to walls than cover them with wallpaper or paint. By introducing mouldings to form dado rails and panelled areas, a wider range of decorative treatments becomes possible. But the application of mouldings does not stop there. They can also be used to transform plain doors, cupboard doors, shelving, mantelpieces and furniture.

In eighteenth-century Europe, delicate and elaborately carved mouldings were used to divide walls into a series of panelled areas, which were sometimes further divided by dado rails. Doors were also divided into panels, echoing the decoration of the walls. The walls were often painted in two or three tones of colour. In very grand rooms the mouldings were picked out in gold or in a lighter toning shade. A similarly elegant arrangement was favoured in the Neo-classical schemes introduced towards the end of the eighteenth century. All the architectural wall decorations – a cornice or stucco-work frieze at the top of the wall, panelling and dado rail – were generally left white against a plain-coloured background. This treatment works just as well in a modern room, particularly if it is rather box-like. By keeping the panels as upright rectangles, the eye is drawn upwards, giving an illusion of height.

Modern mouldings

Modern wooden mouldings can be found in most hardware stores. You may want to buy a plumb-line to help you get the lines absolutely straight. You will also need a mitring block for sawing corners. Paint the areas within the panels either a tone lighter or darker than the main wall

Right: The plain white moulding on the cupboard door gives a distinctly modern feel to this dining room.

colour, and the moulding in a complementary colour. It is always better to paint the panels rather than to cover them in wallpaper.

In the eighteenth century chairs were placed against the wall, so a rail at chair height was a useful way to protect expensive wall decorations from scrapes and bumps. Nowadays, the dado, which is usually positioned at about windowsill height, serves as a means of visually reducing the height of a high wall. An excellent way to use moulding is to create a dado rail and then wallpaper the area above it. Paint everything below the rail either off-white or a colour that tones in with the paper, or add small square or rectangular panels. This treatment is particularly useful along the length of the staircase, which often gets kicked and scuffed. It is much cheaper to paint over these than to re-paper.

You do not have to use wooden mouldings for any of these ideas. Instead you can use paper borders to indicate panels and dados, and of course, you can also use print-room embellishments in the same way (see pages 8–11).

Absolutely plain doors are transformed when they are decorated with mouldings. You can use them to introduce panels, such as a pair of rectangular panels positioned above two smaller square or rectangular panels. Mouldings can also be used on plain cupboard doors to great effect. The edges of undistinguished tables, chairs, stools – anything that offers a straight edge – will all benefit from the addition of a moulded feature.

Panelling a Plain Door

You will need:

- ➤ Plumb-line or tape measure
- ➤ Pencil
- ➤ Wooden rope moulding
- ➤ Small mitring block
- ➤ Small handsaw
- ➤ Re-usable adhesive
- ➤ Wood glue
- ➤ Filler
- ➤ Scraper (to apply filler)
- ➤ 0.5 lt (1 pt) tin of eggshell paint

Method

A

1 In this project, we have made a rectangular panel with an inner diagonal cross. First of all, measure the door and mark out your panel and cross in pencil (**fig A**).

2 You will need to cut four pieces of moulding to make the frame, and one long diagonal piece and two short diagonal pieces for the inner cross. Once you have cut the lengths of moulding with the handsaw, you need to mitre the ends (see page 11). The long diagonal piece needs to be mitred on both sides of both ends. With each of the two short diagonal pieces, mitre the end that goes into the centre of the cross on one side at an angle of less than 45°. The ends of the short diagonal pieces that fit into the corners of the rectangle need to be mitred on both sides (**fig B**).

3 Before sticking down the moulding, attach it with re-usable adhesive to make sure you have positioned it correctly. Once you are sure it all fits together, glue first the rectangular panel and then the inner cross in place (**fig C**). Leave to dry for 24 hours.

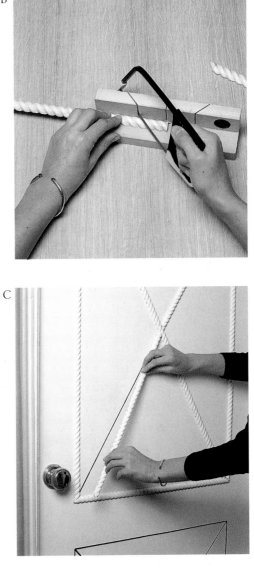

B

C

4 If the pieces of moulding do not fit together quite perfectly (and they probably will not) fill up the cracks with a filler.

5 Once the glue and filler is dry, paint the moulding in the colour of your choice.

FLOORS

Decorating Floors

Many of the decorative paint techniques used on floors and floor coverings in the past are still used today, adapted to make the most of modern materials. One of the simplest and most traditional ways of decorating a floor is to paint the floorboards, using either a plain colour on its own or with the addition of a stencilled design (see pages 44–47), or a paint effect such as marbling.

In the nineteenth century, it was usual to give a paint treatment only to the parts of floorboard that were not covered by carpet. A much more common sight, however, were decorative floorcloths made of canvas and painted with oil paints. In the eighteenth and nineteenth centuries they provided a cheap and colourful alternative to carpeting, and were particularly useful in areas of a house where valuable carpets would have been worn down too quickly. At first, floorcloths were hand-painted to imitate marbling, parquet and tiling. Later, manufactured floor-cloths became fashionable, but they, in their turn, were replaced by a new material, linoleum (see pages 32–35).

Painted mats

Today, when most furniture and household items are ready-made, anything individually crafted has a very special appeal. There are a number of artists in Europe and America who are producing floor paintings to commission. Some of these floor paintings are patterns or stencilled motifs, while others are complicated scenes with

Left: A variety of effects can be achieved by painting matting. Here, plain sisal matting has been stencilled to look like an intricately woven rug.

representational images. If placed on top of a hard floor, they are, like linoleum, very hard-wearing.

As an alternative to these expensive, hand-painted floorcloths, you can paint your own sisal matting. Sisal is a modern product made from the leaves of the *Agave sisalana* plant. There is nothing new about using plant fibres for flooring – in early medieval times, rushes and straw were strewn on the floor, and in summer sweet-smelling herbs and flowers were added to give off a delicious scent as they were trodden down. Gradually, the rush or straw was woven into matting. Various types of matting continued to be used in poorer homes over the centuries, but, in recent years, it has become really fashionable. The superior quality of modern matting, and its lower cost compared to the equivalent in carpets, makes it very attractive.

You can buy sisal matting in a wide variety of natural and dyed colours, and a range of hard-wearing weaves. As sisal matting takes oil paints particularly well, it offers considerable scope for the home decorator.

Decorating sisal matting is very simple – it can be stencilled or painted. For the beginner, bold geometric shapes are the easiest to attempt. Designs based on natural forms such as flowers and leaves are usually more difficult to apply, as curves are more complicated to produce than straight lines. More ambitious schemes, for example, producing painted replicas of antique carpets, are possible in the hands of experienced artists but are probably too difficult for the amateur to achieve.

Sisal floor covering can be used throughout the house, and it provides an excellent base for decorative rugs. Loose sisal mats are also available, and look best finished with a bound edge of jute border. In this project, a single sisal mat is stencilled with simple, but very effective, geometric shapes.

Painting Sisal Matting

You will need:

- Sisal matting cut to the required size. We used a piece of sisal matting 1x1.2 metres (3x4 ft).
- Card
- Pencil
- Scissors
- Masking tape
- Stencil brush
- Red eggshell paint
- Green eggshell paint

Method

1 Work out the inner and outer border. According to the mat's dimensions, cut four strips of masking tape for the outer border and stick them 4 cm (1½ in) in from the edge of the mat. Then measure your inside border. In this example, it is 20 cm (8 in) in from the outer border. Stick a rectangle of masking tape 20 cm (8 in) from the outer border, then leave a gap of 2.5 cm (1 in) and stick another rectangle 23 cm (9 in) in from the outer border.

2 You can make the four-sided stars as large or small as you like. To draw a perfect four-sided star, draw a vertical line

A

and cross it with a horizontal line of equal length. Join up the four points of the cross to make a diamond shape. Measure the halfway point of each side of the diamond and draw a diagonal line through them. Mark the middle point of each of these four diagonal lines and draw lines from the halfway points to the tips of the original diamond shape. You will now have made a perfect four-sided star. Using this method, make one large star and six small stars.

B

C

MORE IDEAS

*If you bind the edges of a
sisal mat, you can add an
extra touch by sticking studs
along the binding
(see pages 16–19).*
❖

3 Cut out the large star and place it in the middle of the inner rectangle. Outline the border of the star with masking tape. Place one small star in each of the four corners and one in the middle of the two long sides of the rectangle. Outline these in masking tape **(fig A)**.

4 With a stencil brush, paint on the borders in red eggshell. Then paint the stars in green eggshell **(fig B)**. Leave to dry for 4 to 6 hours and, when the paint is dry, peel off the masking tape.

5 To make the additional star points, measure halfway down the points of the cut-out stars you have already made and cut off the tips. Stick these tips between the green star points and outline them with masking tape. Stencil in with the red eggshell **(fig C)**. Leave to dry for 4 to 6 hours.

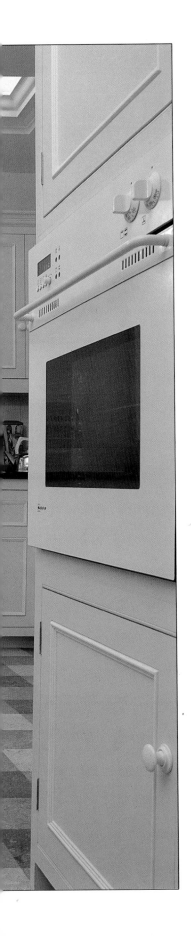

Linoleum

There is a wide range of materials to choose from when it comes to selecting an attractive, tough flooring for areas such as hallways, passageways, kitchens and bathrooms. At the top end of the market there are tiles in marble, terrazzo, brick, ceramic and mosaic, while at the cheaper end, cork and vinyl are the most popular forms of flooring. Linoleum, or lino, is another type of durable flooring that is coming back into fashion. This traditional floor covering was invented by Frederick Walton, an Englishman, in 1863, and its manufacture quickly spread worldwide. Imagine the delight of nineteenth-century householders, who until then had had to make do with oilcloth flooring, which was a canvas painted or stencilled with oil-based paints (see pages 28–31). As one enthusiast of lino commented at the time, it was 'softer and less noisy to walk on than oilcloths and neither cold nor slippery as oilcloths are'.

Until the advent of petrol-based flooring products, lino had no equal, but it lost popularity as the newer vinyl floorings were introduced. In more recent years, however, its positive qualities have been rediscovered. One of the most important from an enviromentally friendly point of view is that it is made entirely from natural substances – a mixture of linseed oil, wood flour and pine resin, the last two being by-products of other industries. This glossy, flexible, hardwearing flooring will withstand cigarette burns, and its anti-bacterial qualities make it very suitable in the kitchen. Lino is available in tiles and sheet form and comes in a wide range of colours (the attractive marbling is caused by the dying process itself). It looks good laid as one colour, but because it is such a supple material, lino is also easy to cut and inlay in almost any design. All-over

Left: Checked linoleum makes an attractive, easy-to-clean and hygienic floor covering, ideal in modern kitchens.

geometrical patterns with straight edges are easiest to put down – curves are tricky to cut and inlay accurately. Borders can also present problems if the room is not absolutely square or rectangular – a border will simply draw attention to any irregularities. Alternatively, you can use ready-cut tiles to create an attractive pattern such as a chequerboard or gingham, which works well in a nursery or kitchen.

Lino Cutting

You will need:
- Red lino tiles
- Blue lino tiles
- Pencil
- Cardboard
- Scissors
- Stanley knife
- Linoleum tile adhesive

Method

1 First make the border. With a ruler measure a 5 cm (2 in) wide border along two sides of the blue tile, about 10 cm (4 in) in from the edge of the tile. Score along the ruler edge with the Stanley knife (fig A). Then remove the two strips. Do the same on the red tile.

2 Draw a four-sided star on the cardboard (see page 30). Cut out the star with the scissors. Place the template onto the centre of the red tile. Score around it with the Stanley knife (fig B). Remove the template and, using the Stanley knife, cut out the lino star. Repeat the process with the blue tile.

3 Place the red strips into the blue tile making a border.

4 Place the cut-out red star into the star shape in the blue tile (fig C).

A
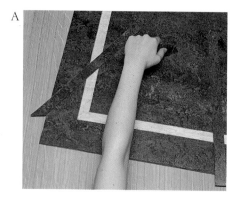

B

C

MORE IDEAS

Linoleum does not have to be confined to floors. It makes a warm and attractive surface for a desk or table top.

❖

Tartan Design

Any type of plaid or check gives a bold and cheerful feel to a room, but the richest and most evocative of all plaids is tartan. An extremely versatile material, it adds warmth and colour to any room. You can be bold and use it extensively with a combination of tartan floor-length curtains together with a tartan carpet, set off by deep red-painted walls. Or you can use just a small amount of tartan to cover a couple of cushions or use as upholstery material for a chair with just as stunning an effect.

Tartan has a history, too. It conjures up images of Bonnie Prince Charlie in full Highland dress, of dark green hills splashed with purple heather and baronial stone halls hung with stags' heads. These images are far from fanciful. In the sixteenth and seventeenth centuries, tartan material was widely used to decorate Highland houses; it was hung on the walls for both decoration and warmth and draped over furniture. Lengths of it were worn as rough, belted kilts, with a trailing end which could be flung over the shoulder, leaving the sword arm free. In the eighteenth century, tartan became an important symbol of unity between Highland and Lowland Scots in their struggle against unification with England.

Today, there are over 700 registered tartans. These are of comparatively recent invention, and owe their existence to Queen Victoria in the late nineteenth century; her almost fanatical adoption of the material and thirst for creating new patterns probably secured its survival. She fell in love with Scotland and its traditions

Left: Tartan creates a rich warm atmosphere and is perfect for a small room like this study.

and ended up by carpeting and curtaining Balmoral (the royal residence in Scotland) in Royal Stewart. By doing so she instigated a fashion for using tartan in interior decoration.

In the early 1980s tartan was picked up by the designer Ralph Lauren, who promoted it as part of his up-market country look. Although 'modern' tartan has taken on a smartness in both dress and decoration, the material still evokes a strong link with heroic Scottish tradition.

A touch of tartan

Tartan has many virtues. It is supremely versatile, will brighten up the dullest corner and is hard-wearing. You can buy it in a variety of weights and in a huge range of colours. Although it looks best in darker rooms, such as a study or dining room, it will go just about anywhere. For people who are tired of chintz, it can be a revelation. In addition, because the material is woven, usually in gentle, subtle shades, there is a softness around the edges of the design where the colours meet. This gives tartan a kind of neutral quality that makes it easy to live with and means that it will blend happily with other colours in almost any decorating scheme. It can look really effective as a throw-over on the back of a sofa or made up into a tablecloth and edged with braid. Tartan ribbon will transform an open shelf unit if you first scallop it, then attach lengths of it to the shelf fronts. Wider tartan ribbon looks wonderful used as trimming round the edges of plain curtains or as a backing for a vertical row of small prints – with a tartan bow on top! Alternatively, you can paint tartan as a design on a piece of furniture.

Painting a Storage Chest in Tartan

You will need:

(For a medium-sized three-drawer chest)

➤ Tape measure
➤ Pencil
➤ Sandpaper
➤ 19 mm ($^3/_4$ in) masking tape
➤ 5 cm (2 in) wide and 6 mm ($^1/_4$ in) wide paintbrushes
➤ 1 lt (2 pt) tin of white wood primer
➤ 1 lt (2 pt) tin of dark grey undercoat (use white undercoat if you are painting a light-coloured tartan)
➤ 1 lt (2 pt) tin of raspberry-coloured, oil-based eggshell paint
➤ 0.5 lt (1 pt) tin of brownish-red, oil-based eggshell paint
➤ 0.5 lt (1 pt) tin of dark green, oil-based eggshell paint
➤ Steel wool
➤ White spirit for cleaning the brushes

Method

It is advisable to work in a well-ventilated room.

1 If you are using a chest of drawers which is already painted or has a varnish or wax finish, sand the chest down first using fine-grain sandpaper.

2 Remove the drawers, and paint the fronts of them and the outside frame with white wood primer. Leave to dry for 16 to 24 hours.

3 Paint over the primer with a coat of grey undercoat. Leave to dry for 6 to 16 hours.

4 Apply the background-colour paint (raspberry) to the drawer fronts and chest. You can use two coats of this if you wish, leaving each coat to dry for 16 to 24 hours.

5 When the background paint is completely dry, use a pencil and tape measure to mark out where the broad, 5 cm (2 in) horizontal stripes will be. Do this by finding the centre of each of the surfaces (sides, top, drawer fronts) and work outwards from there in 5 cm (2 in) sections. Leave a l0 cm (4 in) gap between each 5 cm (2 in) stripe. To make sure the lines stay straight and parallel, mark out a series of dots on the painted surface as a guide.

6 Using masking tape, which it is best to press on with a clean cloth rather than using your fingers, create a grid of horizontal stripes on the chest and drawer fronts.

7 Paint these stripes between the lengths of masking tape in the brownish-red colour, using the 5 cm (2 in) brush. Leave the stripes to dry for 16 to 24 hours, removing the masking tape after 4 hours (fig A).

8 When these first stripes are completely dry, repeat Stages 5 and 6, this time creating vertical 5 cm (2 in) stripes in the same brownish-red colour. Leave to dry for 16 to 24 hours, carefully removing the masking tape after 4 hours (fig B).

A   B   C

9   With a tape measure and pencil, mark out where the thin horizontal green stripes will go. These are 6 mm (¹/₄ in) thick, 2.5 cm (1 in) away from each side of the broad stripes.

10   With masking tape, create a grid for these thin lines, and using the 6 mm (¹/₄ in) brush, paint the green stripes between the lengths of masking tape **(fig C)**. Leave to dry for 16 to 24 hours, removing the masking tape after 4 hours.

11   Repeat Stages 9 and 10, this time to paint in the vertical, thin green stripes.

12   If your chest of drawers has wooden knobs, you can either paint in one of the plain colours or carefully continue the tartan pattern over them.

13   To give a final antique effect, gently brush a handful of fine, steel wool over the painted surface, which should be completely dry. This final technique will give a slightly worn or antique look to the wood.

Instant Furniture Makeovers

Not all decorating ideas can be instantly achieved. Découpage (see pages 56–59), for example, may be a cheap and extremely effective way of giving furniture a completely new look, but it takes time to find suitable patterns or images and then to cut them out, arrange them into a design and stick them down piece by piece. If you like the basic idea of découpage, but not the amount of work involved, use whole sheets of wrapping paper instead to cover furniture. A smart blue paper sprinkled with gold stars or dotted with shells and seaweed is ideal for a small bathroom cabinet. Choose teddy bears, dolls or farmyard animals to cover the top of a small table or chest of drawers in a child's room. Neatly trim the paper to the size and shape of the surface or surfaces to be covered, then glue it on. If you have more time, add a braid trim or paper around the edges as a finishing touch. (Alternatively, using braid or a paper border alone to edge a painted piece of furniture will also give it a quick lift.) To finish, just brush on a couple of coats of matt or gloss varnish.

If you have larger pieces of furniture that need covering, wallpaper is often a good solution. Some of the special paint finish papers work well on furniture, particularly coloured 'faux' effects or sponged or dragged papers for an instant effect. In the seventeenth and eighteenth centuries, it was fashionable to have lacquered chinoiserie furniture (see pages 112–115). If you like this look, try using a modern imitation chinoiserie paper, although this is expensive and painting it would be more durable. It is probably best to varnish over everything once it has been pasted down, but try out the varnish on a sample of your chosen paper first to check if and how it affects the colour – sometimes varnish can cast a yellow tone over colours, which you may not like.

Old music sheets, torn up into long, even strips and pasted down in lines or quite higgedly-piggedly look striking on a small cabinet or shelves. You can also use sheets of plain coloured paper in the same way. Choose one colour, or use two or three subtly toning shades. Newspaper also works well, either torn or left whole and then covered with a dilute coat of paint so that the print still shows through. Again, varnish the finished surface to protect it from bumps.

Right: Transform old furniture by painting it or covering it in brightly coloured wrapping paper.

Decorating a Shelf with Sheet Music

You will need:

- Sheet music
- Access to a photocopier
- Wallpaper paste
- Paintbrush (for paste)
- Satin-finish varnish
- Brush for varnish

Method

1 If your shelf is rough, sand it before you start covering it.

2 Depending on the size of your shelf, photocopy the sheet music enough times to give you an all-over covering of paper.

3 Tear up the photocopies into a variety of shapes **(fig A)**.

4 Mix up the wallpaper paste according to the manufacturer's instructions and, with a brush, carefully apply a layer of paste onto the backs of the torn photocopies. Stick them down, making sure as you do so that the pieces overlap with one another, so that every bit of the shelf will be covered **(fig B)**. It is a good idea to wipe over the paper with a cloth once it is stuck down, pushing out any air bubbles that may be trapped under it.

5 Once the wallpaper paste is dry, varnish over the paper with a satin-finish varnish **(fig C)**. Leave to dry for 6 hours.

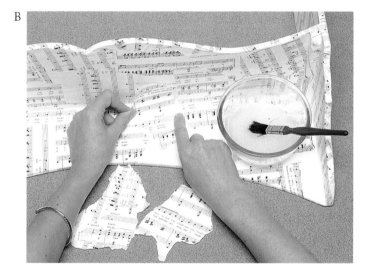

MORE IDEAS

Take some pretty coloured gingham-patterned paper, fold it concertina-style and cut out the shape of a heart using a cardboard template. Use this to form a border around the top of a chest of drawers. Punctuate the drawers with individual heart shapes. You can also use the outlines of birds, animals and flowers in the same way.

❖

Autumn leaves make superb instant decorations. Collect fallen leaves and place them between sheets of newspaper under a pile of books to flatten and dry them off. Arrange and glue them onto your chosen piece, for example, as a border on a tray. Finish with a coat or two of varnish.

Stencilling

Stencilling is a wonderful confidence booster. The technique is straightforward; it simply involves transferring a design by brushing paint into a hollow-cut image in a piece of acetate or card. The easiest way to stencil is to use just one design and one colour, perhaps for a border on a wall, or to frame a door or window. If you find choosing colours difficult, use the same colour as the main wall colour but apply it more thickly. The result is subtle but very effective. Another variation is to alternate several tones of the same colour for your stencil.

The paint can be brushed evenly into the stencil for a perfectly flat look, but a more interesting approach is to carefully load the brush with paint, and start applying the paint with a firm hand at one end of the stencil and then gradually release the pressure as you move along until the brush is barely touching the surface. If you use a natural marine sponge, it will give a marbled effect. Aerosol spray paints make the job quicker, but they can be awkward to control successfully – practice on scraps of paper first and always work in a well-ventilated area. It is a good idea to try out any design on spare paper initially (paint the paper first in the same colour as your background to give you an even clearer impression). Stick the stencilled piece of paper to the proposed site with light-tack masking tape to see how it looks.

You can find ideas for your designs from the past. In colonial America, the early settlers drew inspiration for their stencilled designs from their surroundings, and natural motifs such as native flowers, leaves, fruit, birds and stars brightened up their interiors. If you have the time – and the patience – use stencils to create an all-over wall design, rather like a patterned wallpaper. This was how the first wallpapers were made in France in the seventeenth century, and later in America in the eighteenth century. Early paper came in narrow strips that were painstakingly decorated using several stencils to build up each part of the design. Borders hung vertically and fairly wide apart on plain wallpaper involves less work but creates a similar effect.

At the other end of the scale, you can use stencils more sparingly to provide decorative accents in the tradition of European and American folk art – perhaps one large, multi-coloured stencilled design on the top of a chest of drawers or on the lid of an old chest. Fortunately, modern clear acetate stencils make multiple-coloured stencil designs easy to execute, as they can be placed one on top of the other, and the registration marks are always clearly visible. Ready-made stencils are widely available, but you can also make your own, perhaps picking up on a design featured elsewhere in the room.

Left: You can stencil very simple shapes such as stars and moons, or more
complicated patterns such as these chinoiserie motifs.

Stencilling a Wicker Basket

You will need:

- Wicker basket
- White undercoat paint
- Blue eggshell paint
- 5 cm (2 in) paintbrush
- Card
- Pencil
- Scissors
- Masking tape
- White emulsion paint
- Stencil brush (you can make your own by snipping off the end of an ordinary paintbrush to 2.5 cm (1 in)
- Varnish and brush

Method

1 Make the stencils by cutting the shape of the moon and stars out of card. You can draw these freehand or trace them from a book. Once you have drawn the outline, cut out the shape in the middle (fig A), keeping the piece of card with the hollow image. This is your stencil.

2 Paint the basket in white undercoat and then, when dry, add a coat of blue eggshell, leaving it to dry overnight.

3 Once the paint is dry, attach the stencils with masking tape in a design of your choice (fig B).

4 Using the stencil brush, stencil on the white emulsion in the cut-out images (fig C). Apply the paint sparingly to the brush and dot inside the image lightly. In this way you will produce a textured effect. Leave to dry overnight.

A

B

MORE IDEAS

If you have some plain tiles in the bathroom or kitchen, it is possible to stencil them. Sand over the tiles with a rough sandpaper, dust, then prime with a universal adhesive and sealer. When the sealer has dried, brush on a topcoat of oil-based paint. The tiles are ready for stencilling using oil-based paints. To protect the decoration, varnish over the stencilled tiles.

❖

C

Stamping

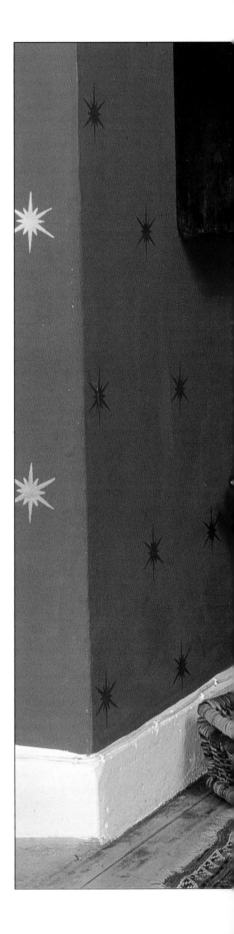

Stamping or block printing was one of the earliest means by which fabrics were decorated mechanically. The method is simple: a relief image is carved onto a wooden block, dipped into ink, paint or dye, and then stamped onto a surface. By the eighteenth century many of the Indian calicoes or 'chints' (a type of early chintz), so sought-after in the West, were block printed in order to meet the huge export demand. Block printing was also widespread in Europe by then, and is still the method preferred by a few specialist fabric firms.

Block printing can be done with vegetables or fruit. Potatoes are a popular medium as they are easy to cut and offer a generous printing surface area, but carrots, turnips and parsnips (although they can be hard to carve) can all be used. Hard fruits, such as apples and pears, give a delicate print when they are halved. Remember to leave the cut area exposed to the air for a few minutes so that it goes brown – this dries out the surface and ensures a good print impression. You can also make an attractive print from ordinary household items such as string or rope. Glue lengths of them onto a wooden block to form an interesting pattern. When you print with them, you will produce a highly textured effect. You can use vegetable or wooden blocks to stamp a wide variety of items, including trays, boxes, furniture, wickerwork and fabric.

Ready-made decorative rubber stamps take all the hard work (or fun, depending on your point of view) out of producing your own prints. The range of ready-made designs has increased greatly since vulcanization (the process by which rubber is moulded to form a stamp) was discovered by Charles Goodyear in the 1860s. At first

Right: Simple shapes, such as stars, make very effective stamps – they are also easy to make.

rubber stamps were used exclusively by the Post Office and were then taken up by offices in general.

The first decorative stamps were made for children as educational toys. You can still buy a wide range of stamps that appeal to children, such as cartoon characters, figures from fairy tales and classic children's stories. For adults the selection is even greater: everything from pretty floral designs, animals, birds and fish to classical motifs and film stars. These are available from craft shops, specialist outlets and by mail order. Special stamp fabric inks are also available for decorating fabric.

Stamping furniture

Before you start, test your stamps on paper first. This is vital, since no two stamps are alike, and you may need to make adjustments to the amount of pressure you apply in order to get a good result. Start with something simple, such as a mirror frame painted a plain colour in eggshell (eggshell offers a good base when it comes to stamping furniture). Place a stamp in the centre of each side, and one in each corner. Probably the easiest design would be flowers or leaves, or some form of geometric pattern. Instead of redecorating a whole room, you could just add a border. Or you could decorate the top of a chest of drawers with a border of stamped images, and perhaps the same stamped design on either side of the handle of each drawer. Chairs, chests, tables, boxes can all be treated in the same way. You can dust on an embossing powder (this comes complete with instructions) when working on furniture – it must be heated briefly (a hair dryer held at a safe distance is fine) to fix it. Always finish with an all-over coat of gloss or matt varnish to protect both the furniture and the stamped image. When varnishing gold images, brush the varnish on very gently, as the gold pigment has a tendency to smear if you are not careful.

Stamping a Chair

You will need:

- ➤ Wooden chair
- ➤ 0.5 lt (1 pt) tin of eggshell paint
- ➤ Paintbrush
- ➤ Card
- ➤ Pencil
- ➤ Scissors
- ➤ Four potatoes cut into halves
- ➤ Kitchen knife or penknife
- ➤ Small tin of black poster paint
- ➤ Small tin of red poster paint
- ➤ Gloss or matt varnish

Method

1 Prepare the chair surface by cleaning it and painting it a plain colour in eggshell paint.

2 On the card, draw the stamp shapes: hearts, clubs, spades and diamonds. Carefully cut out the shapes. We have made large stamps for the chair seat and smaller ones for the frame.

3 Shape each potato half into a square. Place your card cut-out shape on top of the square surface and, with a sharp knife, cut around it **(fig A)**. Remove the card and cut away under the shape at an angle so that you make a 'V' under your stamp. Leave the base of your block square – this is what you hold as you stamp. Make eight stamps; a large heart, diamond, spade and club, and a small set as well.

A

4 Once you have made your stamp shapes, you can start applying them to the chair. Dip each stamp into the poster paint and press it firmly onto the chair surface (**fig B**). Leave to dry for a couple of hours.

5 Once the paint is dry, apply a coat of varnish for protection (**fig C**). Leave to dry overnight.

Cupboard Doors

There are lots of different ideas to choose from when it comes to cupboard doors. One of the most attractive looking is to replace the centre panel of each door with chicken-wire and hardboard, as shown in the project that follows. An undistinguished cupboard is instantly smartened up, and if the panels are already in poor condition, this may be a better and cheaper solution than completely replacing the doors.

Many smaller side cupboards in the eighteenth and nineteenth centuries were constructed along these lines, and were known as chiffoniers. Instead of chicken wire, they had brass grilles for panels, and these were sometimes backed with silk gathered into pleats. Glass was expensive in those days, especially in the eighteenth century, so insetting the doors with grilles was probably an economy measure. Chiffonier fronts are much more commonly found nowadays covering boxed-in radiators – one way of disguising a very necessary twentieth-century innovation. You can, of course, use brass wire for door panels, but chicken-wire looks just as smart. You can either leave the wire absolutely plain, or paint it using an oil-based paint (do not forget to prime it with a metal primer first). Depending on the style of the cupboard and the look you want, choose whether or not to add the hardboard backing – some clothes cupboards in English country houses used chicken-wire alone, and to great effect. Alternatively, a gathered fabric backing looks very stylish. Simply gather and pin the fabric to the back of the door, or sew a narrow casing at top and bottom and thread plastic-covered spring

Left: Replace old cupboard door panels with new ones. It is easy to make your own replacement panels with fabric and chicken wire.

wire through, neatly gathering the fabric as you work along. Hook the ends of each spring wire to rings fixed inside either side of the door panel.

Fabric used in this way also looks good backing functional glass-fronted cupboards. If you choose to add hardboard backing, you can paint the panels a plain colour or apply a special paint effect such as dragging or sponging. Or, alternatively, you can stick on a decorative paper – wrapping paper is ideal as it is cheap, and comes in such a wide range of designs, as does wallpaper. *Trompe-l'oeil* papers are very effective, particularly those with false books or crockery on them.

A number of ideas covered in this book can be applied to cupboards. Use stencils to introduce a border around each door panel, and finish with a central motif (see pages 44–47). A silhouette pasted or painted onto the centre of each panel looks elegant (see pages 108–111). Paint the rest of the door panel off-white, and, if you like, use fine lines to pick out any mouldings in gold paint. Do not overlook architectural detailing for the doors in the form of mouldings (see pages 24–27), rope (see pages 128–131), studs (see pages 116–119), furnishing braid, or even print room decorations (see pages 8–11).

Decorating Cupboard Doors

You will need:

- ‣ Tape measure
- ‣ Hardboard, cut to size
- ‣ Pencil
- ‣ Scissors
- ‣ Wallpaper or wrapping paper
- ‣ Chicken wire
- ‣ Wire cutters
- ‣ Staple gun
- ‣ Glue
- ‣ Nails or some other device for attaching panels to cupboard

Method

1 Measure the panels on your exisiting cupboard and buy hardboard panels to fit.

2 Lay a hardboard panel on top of the wallpaper or wrapping paper, draw around it with a pencil and cut out as many pieces of paper as you need (**fig A**). Glue the paper panels to the hardboard panels (**fig B**).

3 Using the wire cutters, cut the chicken wire 7.5 cm (3 in) larger all round than the hardboard panels.

4 Lay a piece of chicken wire over a hardboard panel and bend the edge of the wire around the panel, stapling to the board (**fig C**). Repeat this for each of the panels. To fix the panels to the door, use nails or brackets. Ask at a DIY store for advice.

A

B

MORE IDEAS

An arrangement of shells looks striking stuck onto a cupboard door. You could stick on a narrow border of shells around the edges. In the centre you could put a single motif, such as a starfish.

❖

Découpage (see pages 56–59) is an excellent way of decorating cupboard doors. In a child's room, you could use a theme such as 'the jungle' or 'the farmyard'.

C

Découpage

Découpage is the art of decorating surfaces with paper cut-outs and varnishing them to give the impression of hand-painting or inlay. It is traditionally used on screens and boxes, but it has vast decorative potential for almost any item and surface.

Découpage became popular as an art around 1700, when it was first imported from China to Europe and was spread by merchants. A century later, reproductions were produced in Italy, where cabinet makers started using prints. It was sometimes known as *l'arte del uomo povero*, or 'poor man's art', which perfectly describes this inexpensive craft and its widespread application. At the time, it was used by Venetian craftsmen as an efficient way to meet the high demand for painted oriental-style lacquer furniture (see pages 112–115). Paper cut-outs of oriental motifs were glued to a lacquered surface and varnish was brushed on until the images took on the richness of the originals.

Its charm spread all over Europe, where the skill of cutting with scissors was already an art-form, and prints were especially produced for it. In France, where it was known as *découper*, it was taken up enthusiastically by the aristocracy in the seventeenth and eighteenth centuries. Even France's infamous Queen Marie-Antoinette tried her hand at it. It was also a popular hobby in England, where, in 1760, a book entitled *Ladies' Amusement* was printed. It contained 1,500 hand-coloured designs of flora and fauna, miniature landscapes, animals, arabesques and other borders.

Potichomania was another popular application of découpage, where paper cut-outs were placed on the inside of glass goods to imitate oriental porcelainware. It can be used to decorate the inside of glass vases, glass table-tops and glass splashbacks in bathrooms and kitchens. You can find good paper pictures and

Right: Découpage can be used to decorate a piece of furniture or, as shown by this table, to completely cover and transform it.

shapes from magazines, greetings cards, wrapping paper, and old catalogues such as seed catalogues. Some museum and craft shops may also sell modern copies of original cut-out print books. You can also hunt out old drawings and prints. If you photocopy these on a colour photocopier they will reproduce more realistically. Alternatively, cut out your own découpage pieces from coloured paper.

Before you start, make a drawing of the object on paper. Arrange the pieces until you are happy with the composition, then trace around the shapes as a guide. Make sure that the surface you are sticking to is smooth and dust-free. The surface may need priming with paint first. Once the cut-out pieces have been stuck down, the whole item should be sealed with varnish so that it lasts.

Découpage Table Top

You will need:

➤ A glass-topped table
➤ Paper patterns or images to cut out. In this project, a piece of fabric has been photocopied.
➤ Scissors
➤ Glue for sticking glass. It must be a glue that dries absolutely clear.
➤ Paintbrush (for applying glue)
➤ Sheet of off-white paper
➤ Pencil

Method

1 Cut out the images carefully (**fig A**) and then arrange them on the glass.

2 Once you are happy with the arrangement, glue the pieces in position face up on the back of the glass using the paintbrush (**fig B**). It is very important that you use clear-drying glue and that you apply it carefully, as you are applying the glue to the side of the cut-outs that will show beneath the glass, so any smudges will spoil the finished piece.

3 Once the images are glued on, take the piece of off-white paper and place the glass table-top over it. Draw around the outside edge with a pencil (**fig C**). Cut around the pencil mark so that you end up with a piece of paper exactly the same size as the glass. Place the sheet of paper between the table and the glass top.

A

B

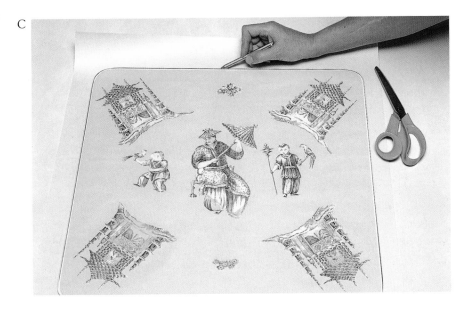

C

MORE IDEAS

You may like to stick to a specific theme when découpaging. You could consider cherubs and hearts, stars and moons, marine life, fruits and flowers, animals and birds, and the seasons.

Edging Shelves

It is easy to give shelving a new life using a range of inexpensive edgings and furnishing trims. In the nineteenth century, if you could not afford to finish off the shelves of your private library with turned mahogany mouldings (the shelves themselves would have been made of a much cheaper wood), you could choose something less expensive and have smart leather edgings stuck on instead. These were made in deep, rich colours such as blues, reds, greens or black and had gilt embossed cutwork – often scallops or inverted triangles. You can still commission authentic edgings like this from specialist suppliers, but they are expensive and you would now be better off using one of the many ready-made mouldings (see pages 24–27) to edge your shelves. You can stain it to resemble a hardwood if you are looking for the strong, luxurious look.

Making your own leather edgings is another possibility. You may be able to find a paper that simulates leather. Use pinking shears to cut out scallops to the required depth, carefully following a template. If you are using leather, you could use a leather hole puncher to punch out evenly spaced holes that echo the line of the cut edge, or use it to introduce some other simple decorative device such as a basic repeating diamond. Remember to leave enough of a lip to glue the leather edging onto the shelf – 5 cm (2 in) is about right.

The cheapest material to edge shelves with is paper. It is also the most flexible. Depending on the paper you choose – anything from wrapping paper to wallpaper –

Left: Lace edging on a shelf looks very pretty, but you can achieve a similar effect by cutting a shaped edging out of paper, ribbon, felt or almost any fabric.

and the design you cut out, the edging can look architectural or lacy, plain or patterned, abstract or figurative. The easiest way to repeat a pattern is to fold the paper concertina-style, draw or trace on the image, then cut it out. Do not try to cut through too many layers of folded paper at once or you may run into trouble keeping clean-cut lines – it is much better to cut out a series of lengths and then discreetly join them together at the back.

Ideas for designs for paper edgings range from the highly intricate to the simple. A geometric design such as a series of small diamonds within larger diamonds looks pretty and is simple to produce, whereas a figurative design such as a series of strutting cockerels is more difficult but very effective. Remember that the colour of the cut-out and the colour of the shelves will also contribute to the fin-ished result. If you want an understated effect, go for a subtle combination, such as white on white, cream on cream or tones of the same colour – for example, a pale blue paper cut-out on shelves paint-ed a slightly deeper colour of the same blue. Contrasts do not have to be loud. White shelves with pastel-coloured edgings look soft and pretty. The deeper and stronger the colour of the cut-out (and the more solid the design) compared to that of the shelf, the bolder it will look.

If you want a really soft effect, use a furnishing trim. Open shelves or shelves in a cupboard in a bedroom would look attractive painted white and then edged with ribbon lace such as a broderie anglaise trim, which is widely available and inexpen-sive. Tartan ribbon would also look very smart with shelves painted dark green or maroon to match.

Edging Shelves

You will need:

- Piece of fabric the length of your shelf and about 7.5 cm (3 in) deep
- Two bottle tops in different sizes
- Pinking shears
- Pencil
- Glue for sticking fabric to wood

Method

1 Place the template of your choice on the strip of fabric, close to one long edge, and draw around it, repeating as many times as necessary **(fig A)**. We have used two alternating sizes of bottle top in our example.

2 Cut around the pencil lines with the pinking shears **(fig B)**.

3 Glue the edging along the shelf **(fig C)**.

A

B

C

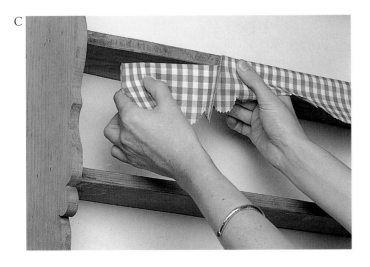

MORE IDEAS

You could follow a particular theme when edging your shelves. For example, you could make a series of farm animals for the kitchen and choose a different geometrically patterned paper for each animal shape, such as stripes, ginghams and diagonals.

❖

Upholstery

Chairs and sofas are very important in a room and it is always worth buying the best quality you can, and then they will last you for life. It is a good idea to make sure that the fabric you choose to cover your sofas and chairs is hard-wearing and will last. Right up until the nineteenth century, seating was for convenience rather than for comfort. Early attempts at upholstery were quite primitive, and consisted simply of putting a pad, made of hair or fur, on top of a hard seat. Later, padding was attached to the bottom frame, which added some, but not much, comfort. In 1828, the invention of coil springs changed all this. By using them with the padding, furniture makers could produce upholstery which would both keep its shape and be infinitely more relaxing to sit on. They stuffed their large and deeply sprung chairs and sofas almost to bursting point, covered them in plush materials, and used heavy buttoning to give an even more sumptuous effect.

Cushions and covers

Today's handmade upholstered furniture is very expensive. It is made traditionally, using cotton wadding, felt, hogshair and natural fibres sprung over a solid beech frame. High-quality cushions are stuffed with duck down and feathers. In less expensive furniture, manufacturers substitute layers of foam for some of these materials. When you are buying furniture like this, try and find out how much foam it contains. Too much, and the arms will literally crumble away so that after only a few years it will need re-upholstering and re-covering. The covering material you decide on is, of course, a matter of individual taste, and there is a large selection of colours, fabrics,

Left: Combine plain and floral-patterned fabrics to create a pretty, colourful, but not overpowering effect.

patterns and textures to choose from. In small sitting rooms a plain, neutral colour will usually look best, while in a library or study, checks, tartans or stripes can be really effective. Larger rooms can take a strong chintz, but you must make sure that it doesn't 'fight' with any other patterns on the walls or carpet. However, this does not mean that all of your upholstered furniture has to be covered in the same material. As long as the fabrics are similar in style and colour tone and meld together, you can

create a pleasing effect by covering one or two of the pieces separately.

Remember that upholstered furniture can always be re-upholstered. This is one of the great things about it – you can change the covering to suit a new colour scheme. Upholstered chairs, in particular those with drop-in seats, are easy to change. You can use them in a dining room or you can transform a hall by arranging two chairs against the wall either side of a table.

Upholstering a Drop-In Seat

You will need:

- Plywood to fit over the frame of the chair seat
- Drill with 8 mm ($^5/_{12}$ in) bit
- Nails
- 1 metre (1 yard) covering material
- Staple gun and staples
- Stanley knife
- 1 metre (1 yard) of 4 cm- (1$^1/_2$ in-) thick foam
- 1 metre (1 yard) cotton wadding

Method

1 Dismantle the drop-in seat, including any webbing, and discard everything but the wooden frame (**fig A**).

2 Cut (or ask your wood merchant to cut) the plywood to the shape of the frame, but make sure it is 1 cm ($^3/_8$ in) smaller all round. You can do this yourself if you make a template of the shape you need and saw the wood carefully so that there are no jagged edges.

3 Drill a few holes in the plywood using an 8 mm ($^5/_{12}$ in) bit. This will allow the upholstery to 'breathe'.

4 Fix the plywood to the frame with nails at 10 cm (4 in) intervals.

5 Put the frame on top of the foam, mark round it in pencil, and cut the foam along the lines with a Stanley knife so that you get a piece of foam 1.3 cm ($^1/_2$ in) bigger than the frame. Lay the foam on top of the plywood.

6 Cut the cotton wadding to a size that is large enough to go over the foam with a little bit to spare.

7 Place the cotton wadding centrally over the foam, pull over the edges, and using the staple gun, attach it to the sides of the frame (**fig B**).

8 Cut to size the material you are using to cover the chair seat, making sure you have cut out enough material for Step 9.

9 Place the material centrally over the seat on top of the cotton wadding. Pull it firmly over the sides, folding it at the corners, and attach it to the underside of the frame with the staple gun (**fig C**).

A

B

MORE IDEAS

Before you buy a piece of upholstered furniture, test how well it has been made by taking out the cushions and sitting on the base. The best sofas have a sprung edge.

❖

Rather than buying expensive furniture from a department store, it can be much more rewarding to look for chairs and sofas in auction rooms or junk shops. Have them professionally restored or do it yourself.

❖

Why not give a new lease of life to an old armchair or sofa, without going to the expense of re-covering it? Instead, use a throw-over such as a shawl or rug.

10 If you want a really professional finish, cut a piece of hessian to the size of the frame. Turn it in along the edges, and staple it to the underside of the seat, punching a hole in the hessian where the dowel comes up from the chair frame to anchor the drop-in seat to the chair.

C

Storage

Storage is often a problem. In particular, it is hard to know where to store things in a neat and attractive way. Here are some suggestions that are both practical and decorative.

A screen is very useful for blocking out unattractive storage boxes with no place to go. Cover the screen with fabric or paint, or découpage it (see pages 56–59). You can make your own screen out of three rectangular wooden frames (preferably hardboard) held together by a series of hinges, and with a cheap fabric, such as calico, stretched over. This part of the operation is made easier if you use a staple gun, otherwise use small nails to hold the fabric in place at the back of the frames. For a more luxurious look, take double the amount of fabric needed to cover the screen and gather it as you go. If you want to prepare the screen for découpage, prime the calico with an acrylic primer or a thinned coat of emulsion, then brush on one or two coats of emulsion to give it a lovely smooth surface on which to work (you can also use an oil-based primer and oil paints to cover the calico). Alternatively, or in addition, stretch elastic or ribbon across to form a network of criss-crosses in which to insert and store notes, letters and cards as shown the following project.

You can also use a screen to form a cupboard or closet in one corner of a room. As well as the screen, you will need a piece of wood cut into the shape of a triangle that fits neatly into the corner space; secure to this a length of clothes rail running from front to back. Use strong angled wall-brackets to install this arrangement securely, and make sure it is just below the height of your screen. All that now remains to be done is to position your screen in

Right: Turn storage space into a feature, as in this child's room, where the cupboard is painted to imitate the facade of red-brick house.

front. If you want 'doors', place a pair of two-panelled matching screens side-by-side, hinged so that the inner panels open outwards. Alternatively fabric can be used instead, in the form of a pair of curtains hung onto curtain track fixed to the front of the triangle.

A chest or trunk is an invaluable storage item. This was one of the few pieces of furniture no medieval household of any standing would be without, and if it was no more than plain and stout, it was undoubtedly serviceable. By the fifteenth century, a wealthy bride always brought a magnificent wedding chest (known as a *cassoni*) to her new home. This was often sumptuously carved and then painted with pastoral scenes. But the dowry chests that will probably inspire you to get out your paints are those decorated by the Pennsylvanian Germans in America. These were hand-painted with traditional folk art motifs, such as as mermaids, unicorns, griffins, or the tree-of-life and hearts, and had plain or combed backgrounds. A combed effect on its own looks good on a wooden or tin trunk. Whether painted, stencilled or découpaged, a chest is always useful and can double as a low coffee or side table or, if it is strong enough, as a seat, with cushions to make it comfortable.

Decorating a Trunk

You will need:

➤ Tin trunk
➤ 1 lt (2 pt) tin of grey undercoat
➤ 1 lt (2 pt) tin of green eggshell paint
➤ Paintbrush
➤ Old credit card
➤ Scissors
➤ 1 lt (2 pt) tin of black eggshell paint

Method

1 Paint the trunk in grey undercoat. Leave to dry overnight.

2 Paint over the trunk with the green eggshell. Leave to dry overnight (**fig A**).

3 With the scissors, cut a serrated edge along the credit card to make a comb.

4 Paint over the green paint with the black eggshell (**fig B**). Quickly, before it dries, drag the comb down over the green paint, creating a wavy line effect (**fig C**). Leave to dry for 16 hours.

Screen with Ribbons

You will need:

➤ Screen
➤ Length of ribbon, 2.5 cm (1 in) wide
➤ Scissors
➤ Staples and staple gun
➤ Needle and thread

Method

1 Measure each panel of the screen and divide it into four sections with a pencil line. Each of these sections will have a diagonal cross of ribbon. Work out how much ribbon you require to create the criss-cross effect. Cut out eight lengths of ribbon.

2 Start at the top of the screen. Hold one piece of the ribbon to one corner, tuck 1 cm ($3/8$ in) of ribbon over the corner and staple it down. Pull the other end of the ribbon diagonally across a quarter of the screen, keeping it taut. Tuck 1 cm ($3/8$ in) of ribbon behind the screen and staple it down. Repeat this over the four sections of the screen. Then repeat from the other side to create the cross.

3 With the needle and thread, sew a couple of stitches in the centre of each cross, attaching it to the screen.

Decorating a Boy's Room

The ideal child's room is both practical and fun. Essentially, this means that whatever decorative elements you introduce, choose surfaces that can be easily cleaned and fabrics that are hardwearing. Always make sure that there is plenty of space for storing toys and clothes.

When it comes to the decor, strong patterns such as stripes or zig-zags are a popular choice for boys. For floor coverings choose a cord carpet, cushioned vinyl or linoleum. Plain floors can be brightened up by coloured rugs, which come in all sorts of designs – from cars and trains to Disney characters and dinosaurs. If you put rugs over vinyl or linoleum, make sure you buy a non-slip backing to avoid accidents.

When choosing curtains, remember that you can buy a special lining to keep the heat in and the sun out; also bear in mind that a design that was absolutely right, with its teddy bears and talking trains, for a four-year-old, will not be appreciated by a seven-year-old. When choosing wallpaper, it is worth noting that while pictorial designs are excellent for stimulating a small child's interest, older boys will probably prefer a simple check or stripe. If you decide on paint, don't cover all the walls in a dark colour as this may prove claustrophobic. Also, many children will treat their walls with little respect, seeing them as a convenient notice-board for their posters and

Left: From the soldier lampstand and colourful duvet cover to the personalized bedhead, this room will enchant any young child.

photographs. So, it is probably a good idea to provide a real noticeboard to minimize the damage!

Painted furniture is an excellent idea for a child's room. Tables, chairs, bookcases or a chest of drawers can be painted with a design of the child's choosing (see pages 80–83). It can always be repainted as the child grows up. When choosing a bed, although they may be more expensive, bunk beds have the merit of being extremely useful when friends stay overnight; they are also space saving and, of course, fun. If you have bunk beds, it is a good idea to fix individual wall lights for both top and bottom bunks, so that one child can read without disturbing the other's sleep. If you choose a single bed, you can create a specialized bedhead, such as the one in the following project.

Racing-Car Bedhead

You will need:

- ➤ Plain wooden bedhead
- ➤ Fine sandpaper
- ➤ Soapy warm water and cloth
- ➤ Small tin of grey undercoat
- ➤ Small tin of matt black eggshell paint
- ➤ Medium-sized paintbrush
- ➤ 4 metres (4 yards) of 7.5 cm- (3 in-) wide black-and-white check ribbon or paper border
- ➤ Colour pictures of cars from posters or glossy motoring magazines. It is important that the paper is thick rather than flimsy, as the latter is difficult to glue and will tear easily.
- ➤ Scissors
- ➤ Re-usable adhesive
- ➤ Wallpaper glue and fabric glue (if you are using ribbon)
- ➤ Small tin of clear satin varnish

Method

1 Sand the bedhead down to remove all varnish and create a smooth surface.

2 Wash the surface lightly with warm soapy water. Wipe it clean and leave until the wood is completely dry.

3 Using a medium-sized paintbrush, apply a coat of grey undercoat to the bedhead. Leave it to dry for 12 to 16 hours.

4 With the same brush paint the bedhead all over, including the sides, with matt black eggshell. Leave to dry for 24 hours.

5 Cut the ribbon or paper border into four lengths, two long and two short, to fit along the sides of the bedhead exactly. If the width of your border is much less than 7.5 cm (3 in), you will need a double width to create the right effect (fig A).

6 Carefully and thoroughly apply the glue to the surface of the border, and stick the lengths one at a time round the edges of the bedhead, overlapping them at each corner.

A

B

7 Cut out the cars carefully (**fig B**). Decide on the arrangement you are going to have for the cut-out cars. You can use one big one, lots of little ones, or a combination of the two. Make sure that your design will fit in the space within the border before you start sticking the cars to the bedhead.

8 Attach the cut-out cars to the bedhead with the re-usable adhesive. Once you are sure they are positioned correctly, stick them on with the wallpaper glue, making sure you cover the backs of the cut-out cars all over. Firmly press the cars onto the bedhead, smoothing each one out so there are no air bubbles or creases (**fig C**). Leave for 24 hours so that the glue has plenty of time to harden.

9 Finally, with the medium-sized paintbrush, apply a coat of clear satin varnish over the cars and the sides of the bedhead, but not over the ribbon. Leave for a further 12 hours, or until the varnish is completely dry.

C

Decorating a Girl's Room

Most girls have definite ideas on how they want their room to look. So before you begin decorating, you should consult your 'client' first. Most girls, though not all, will want the final effect to be pretty and feminine, probably with pastel colours and lots of attractive details.

Plain white walls can be stamped or stencilled. You can either buy kits for doing this or you can make your own. Kits come in a wealth of designs, from flowers to sea-horses. If you want to make your own stencils, cut the shapes out of stiff cardboard or sheets of acetate and attach them to the wall with masking tape. Using a stencil brush and paint, or a can of spray paint, paint inside the cut-out shape. There are also many wallpapers that are suitable for a girl's room. You may like to choose a gingham paper, which comes in a variety of pastel shades, including pink, blue and yellow.

Curtains can bring an extra element of colour and pattern into a room. However, very bright or heavy designs may dominate a room. Pretty lined or unlined voile curtains always look good, as do simple blinds made out of gingham with a frill added to the edges.

When girls are young, they have masses of toys; as they grow older, this turns into piles of clothes. So be sure, when you are planning furniture, to buy a large enough wardrobe. You can paint the wardrobe in a soft colour to

Right: Here, a very pretty effect is achieved by matching the blue-and-white gingham wallpaper with the blue-and-white gingham drapes and canopy of the four-poster cot.

match the room and then stencil on bunches of flowers. Instead of a wardrobe, you can hang a rail with a curtain across a corner of the room. For younger girls, leave a corner of the room clear so that they can create a 'home' area where they can have tea parties with dolls, play games with friends, or make a toy shop. For older girls, if the room is large enough, find an old sofa which you can cover with a throw-over. It will be a great place for your child to curl up and read her books. If she enjoys drawing, keep all the crayons together in some decorated jars. A towel with her name sewn on it, a hairbrush with a hand-painted back or a colourful fabric coat-hanger will all be treasured, and a pretty bedspread, which you can either buy or make yourself, may even encourage her to make her bed.

Gingham Ribbon Bedspread

You will need:

- Calico material large enough to cover the bed with overhang at the sides and bottom. (If one piece is not wide enough, sew together two pieces of calico, using plain flat seams.)
- Tape measure
- Soft pencil
- Pins
- Strong pale cream sewing thread
- Sewing machine
- Quantity of pink gingham ribbon 5cm (2 in) wide. The amount you need will depend on both the size of the bedspread and the squares. As a guide, for a 1.8x2.4 metres (6x8 ft) bedspread you will need 21 metres (21 yards) of ribbon if you are going to sew 60 cm (2 ft) squares, and 37 metres (37 yards) if you decide on 30 cm (1 ft) squares.
- Piece of lining material 2.5 cm (1 in) larger all round than the calico

Method

1 Knowing the dimensions of the material, first work out on paper what size your squares of ribbon are going to be. You should take into account the fact that the smaller the squares, the more ribbon you will need, and also that you will be using a border of ribbon all round the bedspread edges.

2 Lay the calico material flat on the floor, and with the help of a tape measure transfer the grid system you have worked out on paper onto the material, drawing the lines faintly with a soft pencil (fig A).

3 Cut as many strips of ribbon as you need to go on the bedspread lengthwise, and pin them to the calico along the marked-out lines.

4 Cut as many strips of ribbon as you need to go across the width of the bedspread. Weave these alternately over and under the long strips, as if you were darning, and pin them to the calico (fig B).

A

B

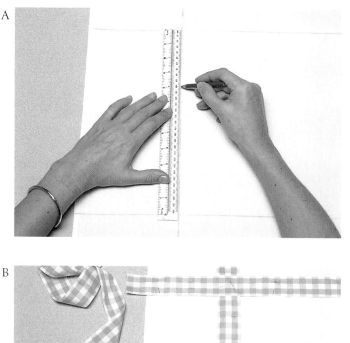

5 When the pattern of squares is complete, sew the ribbon to the calico by machine (fig C). Machine on the border at the same time as sewing on the lining. The calico should overlap the lining by 2.5 cm (1 in) all round.

C

MORE IDEAS

❖

*Make two tails from a material of your choice to represent the
trailing ribbons of a bow. Sew them together to form an inverted
'V' shape, then staple them to a wall. Make a bow out of the same
material and attach this to the wall so that it covers the staples.*

❖

*To contain the clutter of hair slides and jewellery, invest
in a small wicker basket, which you can decorate with ribbons
and bows.*

❖

*Use any left-over ribbon to trim small plain white cushions
to place on the bed during the day.*

Painted Furniture

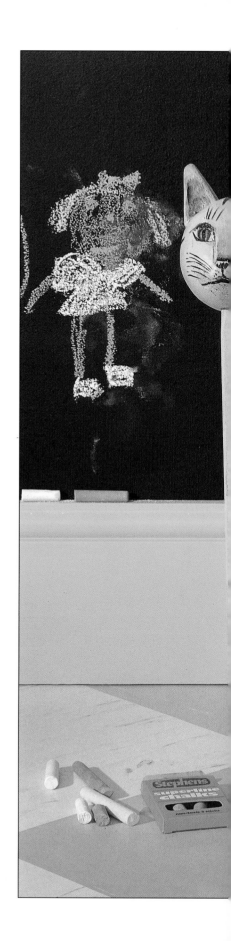

Painting furniture is enormous fun. You can really let your imagination run wild and completely transform, for example, a plain table or an old chest of drawers. It is an ancient art, and examples can be seen in the skilfully painted furniture of cultures as far apart as the ancient Egyptains and the early American settlers.

Producing good painted furniture requires time, patience and planning. With old furniture, in particular, you must make sure you sand off all the varnish first, and give it a good coat or two of undercoat and base colour before you start being creative. It is a good idea to take your choice of colours or theme from the decoration of the room into which the piece of furniture is to go. For example, you can paint a small coffee table to echo the pattern of the wallpaper or fabrics. A more ambitious project is to create a false bookcase on a plain-fronted cupboard by painting in rows of book spines. It will look more effective if you fix chicken wire over the front.

If you do not feel confident enough to tackle a large piece of furniture, you could start with a small wooden lamp base. Paint or stencil it with flowers and then cover it in a layer of varnish for protection. Or you could paint it a subtle terracotta colour and add a design in a darker shade to give it an antique look. Fun-painted furniture fits particularly well into children's rooms. In this project, a small, round wooden table is painted to look like the section through a watermelon.

Right: Painted furniture can be as simple as a chest of drawers decorated with a floral motif or as ambitious as this imaginative yellow and blue 'cat' chair.

Painting a Watermelon Table

You will need:

- Small wooden table with a round top
- Watermelon
- Fine sandpaper
- Palette
- Artist's oil brush, no 4
- Small tin of white undercoat
- Small tin of white eggshell paint
- Pencil
- 7.5 cm (3 in) paintbrush
- Tube of yellow-green artist's oil colour
- Tube of dark green artist's oil colour
- Tube of white artist's oil colour
- Tube of deep pink-red artist's oil colour
- Soft cloth
- Tube of brown artist's oil colour
- Small tin of matt or gloss varnish

Method

1 Cut the fruit vertically in half to copy the fruit section from.

2 Sand down the top and side edge of the table with fine sandpaper, until you have removed all the varnish and the surface is smooth.

3 Using the 7.5 cm (3 in) paintbrush, paint the top and side edge with white undercoat. Leave to dry for 12 to 16 hours.

4 When the undercoat is completely dry, paint over with white eggshell. Leave to dry for 24 hours.

5 Mark out a 6 cm (2 in) band in pencil. Squeeze some of the yellow-green artist's oil colour onto a palette and paint a 6 cm (2 in) band of this round the edge and side of the table top. When you are painting the part of the band which is closest to the centre, use lighter strokes so that the colour is paler. Leave to dry for 16 to 24 hours. Squeeze some of the dark green artist's oil colour onto the palette, and using the artist's oil brush, carefully paint a 1.3 cm (½ in) band round the outside edge of the table, continuing this colour round the sides, to create the effect of the melon's skin (**fig A**). Leave to dry for 16 to 24 hours.

6 Mix the deep pink-red and the white artist's oil paint together to get the right shade of pink and apply this colour at random inside the yellow band (**fig B**). While this paint is still wet, use a cloth to remove some of the paint, creating a stippled effect. Take as much of the paint as you can off the sponge each time you have applied it, or you will find yourself removing it from one part and putting it back on another. Leave this coat for 24 hours, or until it is dry.

7 Using the section of real fruit as a guide, sketch onto the surface of the painted watermelon with a pencil where the segment lines and pips are to go.

A

B

8 With the artist's oil brush, paint in the segment lines with the pink-red oil colour, and paint a small circle of this colour in the middle to form the centre of the fruit.

9 Again using the artist's oil brush, use the white oil colour to stipple lightly, in broken lines, all over the pink section, including the segment lines. This gives a softer and more realistic result. Leave to dry.

10 Squeeze some brown artist's oil colour onto the palette, and using your real fruit segment for reference, paint in the seeds (**fig C**). To make these more realistic, first use a paler brown, by mixing the brown with a little white, and then use the brown on its own to edge one end of each seed. Leave the table to dry for at least 24 hours.

11 When all the paint is completely dry, finish off with a coat of matt varnish over the top and side edges. Leave this to dry for a further 12 hours.

C

MORE IDEAS

When you are using artist's oil colours, it is a good idea to add a few drops of a quick-drying agent to them, available from most paint shops.

❖

Gently rubbing over painted furniture with wire wool will give it an antique effect. However, with this technique you must use an oil-based paint.

Tole

Tole is the art of decorative painting on metal. The word 'tole' is French for sheet iron, and it was from sheet iron that the earliest examples of decorated metalware were made. It dates back to seventeenth-century Europe, when trade with the Far East was flourishing. For the first time Europeans came into contact with imported Japanese and Chinese objects, beautifully decorated with ornamental lacquerwork. They were an immediate success, and demand soon outweighed supply. As the pieces were extremely expensive, European craftsmen began to copy the techniques and style of the oriental lacquerwork onto metal household objects, using a process whereby paint could be applied decoratively to tin.

This painted tinware became particularly fashionable for items such as containers for tea, coffee and chocolate. In the late seventeenth century, most coffee houses stored their beverages in painted tinware boxes. They were hygienic, cheap and practical, but above all they were attractive to look at and would brighten up an interior in a way that earthenware pots could never do.

By the eighteenth century, tole was being used extensively. Amongst other objects it was made into lanterns, candlesticks, vases, trays, clocks, birdcages, hat boxes and inkstands. However, like many fashions, it eventually lost its popularity and there is now very little of this antique tole around, so if you come across a piece, hang on to it; tole items are highly collectable and can be worth almost as much as the oriental lacquerwork they originally copied. Not surprisingly, tole has become popular once again. Made using traditional methods and designs, it is

Left: Paint an item of toleware to match a particular piece of furniture, like this cache-pot which echoes the pink-and-white stripes of the chair.

possible that pieces of modern hand-painted reproduction tole could be the valuable antiques of the future. However, for the present, just one or two of these attractive reproductions, such as a wastepaper basket or wall sconce, can make all the difference to the look of a room.

Colours and uses

The metal is moulded into attractive shapes, sometimes with pierced or scalloped edges, giving toleware a delicate appearance, very different to that of painted wood, which is much heavier. It also comes in a wonderful variety of colours – from dark greens, reds and blues to creams and pastels, all

beautifully decorated, and with a rich, effective use of gold paint either in the applied design itself or as a contrast round the rim.

There is a huge variety of choice in toleware objects – from intricate picture hooks and napkin rings to large trays and elaborate urns. Tole lampshades are especially pretty, used either on candlestick bases or as hanging shades; these can add a distinctive touch, particularly to a hall, bathroom or kitchen. One of the most popular uses of tole is for cache-pots, the French name for plant holders, or planters as they are sometimes called. A prettily painted cache-pot can transform the most boring plant into something rather splendid.

Painting a Cache-Pot

You will need:

➤ Plain metal cache-pot/planter – preferably with a decorative rim

➤ Small tin of light grey metal primer (substitute white primer if you want to use pale colours)

➤ Small tin of dark red eggshell paint

➤ Small tin of dark green eggshell paint

➤ Quantity of stick-on paper stars (depending on the number of stars you want in your decoration)

➤ l9 mm (³/4 in) masking tape.

➤ Good quality 5 cm (2 in) paintbrush

➤ White spirit for cleaning brushes

➤ Clean soft cloth

Method

1 Using the 5 cm (2 in) brush, paint the outside of the cache-pot with metal primer. Leave it to dry for at least l6 hours.

2 Using the same brush, cover the primer with a coat of dark red eggshell paint (fig A). You can use two coats of this if you wish, leaving each coat to dry for l6 to 24 hours.

3 When the red paint is completely dry, attach vertical strips of masking tape at regular 5 cm (2 in) intervals round the outside of the cache-pot over the red paint. Decorate the spaces in between these strips with stick-on stars. After you stick on the masking tape and stars wipe over the edges with a clean cloth, to make sure they are completely stuck down. This will prevent any seepage when the next layer of paint is applied.

A
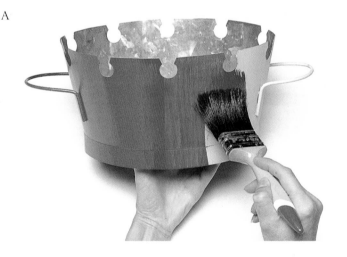

4 When you have checked that the strips and stars are firmly attached, carefully apply the green eggshell paint all over the cache-pot. You don't have to paint over all the masking tape as long as you make sure the edges are covered with green, but it is a good idea to paint over the stars so that you get a clear definition of their shape (fig B). Leave to dry for 24 hours.

5 Carefully peel off the masking tape and stars to reveal the red pattern underneath (fig C).

B

C

MORE IDEAS

Instead of using a cache-pot, decorate a watering can. This looks very attractive standing on the floor. For extra effect, paint the star shapes and sprinkler head in gold.

87

Shellwork

Beachcombing for shells is one of life's simpler pleasures. Walking along the sand at low tide, you can find a wide variety of collectable shells. Once home, however, what do you do with them? In the eighteenth and nineteenth centuries, they would have been displayed in collectors' cabinets, used to decorate walls and ceilings to form a grotto, made into pictures, and used to adorn frames or boxes. Collectors' cabinets are an expensive item these days, but an equally attractive way to display your finest shell specimens on the wall is in a shadow box lined with fabric, preferably one that has a clip-on glass front to keep off the dust. Or you could make a 'Sailor's Valentine'. These were popular in the nineteenth century and consisted of an open container divided into compartments in which shells were laid out in patterns with a central motif, such as a heart, in each compartment. The heart was usually made up of small overlapping shells surrounded by a wide, circular border of shells. The circle was divided into segments, each one containing a different species of shell laid out in horizontal or vertical rows. You can make a 'Sailor's Valentine' with, for example, a hexagonally-sided chocolate box. Cover it with a suitable paper or fabric and then glue in the shells.

Shells are a perfect medium for mosaic work. The Romans created mosaics on fountains and the walls of grottoes. These features were later taken up by the Renaissance Italians. From Italy, the fashion for extravagant grottoes complete with fabulous shell designs, petrifications, crystals and rockwork spread to France and England and later to Germany. Grotto shellwork in particular was a source of inspiration for the exuberant Rococo style that dominated interior design during the eighteenth century in Europe. In the shell pavilion at Goodwood Park, Sussex, England, the Duchess of Richmond and her two daughters took seven years to decorate every bit of the interior with shells.

Grottoes and friezes

The creation of a whole grotto, although perfectly possible, is an enormous task. First of all, you need a vast quantity of shells. If you are interested in making a grotto and are not able to collect your own shells, try any good craft shop or shell mail-order service. A bathroom is a suitably watery location for a grotto (in fact, many shell grottoes included a fountain or pool). A simpler version is to create a

Right: A shell tie-back is ideal for a bathroom window treatment.

shell frieze along all four walls of a room.

A shell mosaic on a piece of hardboard makes a fine decorative panel for a wall. Indeed, any flat surface is suitable for this treatment, for example, doors, cabinets, chests, or even a side table. Whatever the scale of the project, take time planning your design and do not be too ambitious. For inspiration and ideas look at examples of past shell work. You will discover, as ever, that the most successful schemes are also usually the simplest.

Above: Here, shells are used effectively and imaginatively. The simple shell frieze on top of the four-poster frame echoes the shape of the 'shell' chair.

Shell Mirror

You will need:
- ➤ Framed mirror
- ➤ Selection of shells
- ➤ Glue (special glue, obtainable from a craft shop)
- ➤ Varnish

Method

1 Wash the mirror frame with soap and water. Dry it well.

2 Plan your shell pattern by laying out the shells around the outside of the frame or by drawing a design beforehand **(fig A)**.

3 If your frame already has a mirror in it, cover the mirror glass with newspaper to protect it.

4 Cover the frame with glue and stick on your shells carefully following the pre-planned design. It is a good idea to stick on the large shells first **(fig B)**.

5 Varnish the shells for protection **(fig C)**.

A

B

C

MORE IDEAS

*Stick shells on boxes and
photograph frames.*

❖

*Transform old flowerpots by
covering them with shells.*

Papier Mâché

Papier mâché is a simple, tough and wonderfully versatile medium. In the eighteenth and nineteenth centuries, manufacturers produced a wide variety of papier mâché goods ranging from trays and boxes to furniture and architectural ornamental features, such as ceiling roses and panelling. Amazingly, in Australia in the nineteenth century, an attempt was made to make an entire village from papier mâché.

The decorative possibilities are even wider. Traditional papier mâché treatments encompass everything from the lacquerwork so popular in the nineteenth century, which drew on Chinese motifs for its inspiration (see pages 112–115), to the exuberant designs and colours of folk art artefacts from Mexico and India.

The technique – applying strips of pasted paper or paper pulp to a form or mould – has not changed since the Chinese discovered how to make paper in about 200 AD, and then found a way to recycle valuable scraps. This new product proved to be so light, yet tough, that it was used by the Chinese to make their war helmets; in fact, these same properties make it ideal for creating trays, bowls, plates, frames and other decorative objects for the home.

One of the easiest ways to get started with papier mâché is to use it to rejuvenate an old, scratched tray, table or a mirror or picture frame. Once the surface has been covered with papier mâché, it can be decorated. If you prefer to create a new object, a surprising number of

Left: This antique papier mâché table has been painted and varnished to look like black-and-gold lacquerwork.

everyday items can be used for moulds: pudding basins, bowls, baking tins, trays, baskets, margarine tubs and plates are just some of the possibilites. You can even use pieces of fruit or vegetables such as pineapples and pumpkins as moulds. You will find that they make striking and unusual ornaments.

Decorative options

Now to the fun part – the decoration. If you are unsure of your artistic ability, a simple but effective finish is to stick on layers of tissue paper over a plain base colour, finishing with a coat of varnish or lacquer to protect the surface. Sticking on paper cut-outs also works well. If you want to produce a floral design on your finished papier mâché, you will find that wrapping paper is a good source of images. Paint techniques, such as ragging, sponging, combing and spattering require little skill but are very impressive. Or you can try reliefwork on decorative objects – this might be as simple as sticking on string, rope, cardboard cut-outs, or shells and stones, which you can then paint.

If you want to create your own design, work it out on paper first and then transfer it to the papier mâché form using tracing paper. For ideas, you will find inspiration everywhere, but a good place to start is with wallpaper and fabric patterns, books on crafts and the decorative arts, and, of course exhibitions and museums.

To begin, try making something simple, such as a papier mâché bowl.

Papier Mâché Bowl

You will need:

- ➤ One black-and-white newspaper
- ➤ One coloured paper newspaper
- ➤ 0.5 lt (1 pt) wallpaper paste
- ➤ One balloon
- ➤ Mixing bowl
- ➤ Washing-up liquid
- ➤ 2.5 cm (1 in) paintbrush
- ➤ Pencil
- ➤ Scissors
- ➤ Small tin of white undercoat paint
- ➤ Small tin of dark blue gloss paint
- ➤ Small tin of gold paint
- ➤ Gold paper stars
- ➤ Gloss varnish
- ➤ Three dark blue beads

Method

1 Tear about half of the black-and-white and half of the coloured newspapers into approximately 5 cm (2 in) squares.

2 Mix up the wallpaper paste according to the packet instructions.

3 Blow up the balloon. Place it in a bowl or saucepan, and cover it with a layer of washing-up liquid.

4 Apply the first layer of newspaper over the balloon, then add the paste with the paintbrush and then the next layer of paper (**fig A**). The point of using different coloured paper is so that you can tell which layer is which. Eight layers in all are required. Do not try to get an even surface – it is impossible to achieve this with papier mâché. Leave it to dry for about 3 to 4 days in a room where the temperature is steady. This should prevent the balloon from sinking.

5 Burst the balloon with a pin. Place over the papier mâché a bowl of similar size to the one you want to make and draw around the top edge with a pencil. Then remove the bowl and cut around the pencil marking with scissors (**fig B**).

A

B

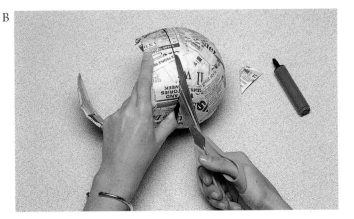

C

6 To produce a smooth edge, cover the rim with a couple of layers of papier mâché.

7 Apply three coats of white undercoat to the surface with a 2.5 cm (1 in) paintbrush. Allow the paint to dry between each coat. Then paint on a coat of dark blue gloss paint (fig C).

8 To decorate the bowl, paint a thin line of gold paint around the inner and outer rim. Stick some gold paper stars onto the outer surface of the bowl. Apply two coats of varnish to all surfaces and leave to dry overnight.

9 Stick three beads in a triangle to the bottom of the bowl – they will help it to sit properly. You can either buy the beads in the appropriate colour or you can paint them yourself.

MORE IDEAS

If you are using fruit or vegetables as moulds, you will need to cover the mould with vaseline so that once the papier mâché is set you can remove it easily. You will then have to apply another couple of layers of papier mâché so that you can paint the finished item.

Lampshades

There are various methods you can use to decorate plain modern fabric or card lampshades. In the nineteenth century, lampshades were made of fabric trimmed with gathered silk or lace, or hung with fringes around the base. If you like this look, you can add a broderie anglaise or lace trim to a plain fabric lampshade or use a piece of lace to cover the whole shade. Tuck a very small hem of lace over the top of the shade and glue it in place. It looks pretty if you allow the lace to fall below the bottom edge of the shade. Alternatively, you can cover a bare strutted frame with lace lined in a plain fabric, which has been gathered with ribbon at the top and bottom. Secure the covering to the frame by sewing the inner lining fabric to the top and bottom rings.

By the 1920s, lampshades made of parchment or vellum were very popular. These were often hand-painted with landscapes or seascapes, or had a scenic print stuck centrally to the front of the shade. Modern card and card-backed fabric lampshades can be treated in the same way using either acrylic or oil-based paints. As the project that follows shows, animal-skin markings are easy to simulate – you could also try tiger stripes or leopard spots. Alternatively, ready-cut clear acetate stencils are flexible enough to be used on the curve of a lampshade, and there are plenty of good designs to choose from (see pages 44–47). An even easier option is to stick cut-outs onto the shade. This could be a print or images taken from wrapping paper or wallpaper (do not forget, you can always increase or decrease the size of the image on a black-and-white or colour photocopier).

Left: These painted lampshades echo the delicate elegance of the decorative features of this dining room.

Another easy way to transform a lampshade is to introduce some form of trimming at the top and bottom of the shade, such as a braid, rope or fringe. This can either match the colour of the shade, or you can use it to provide contrast. For example, if your colour scheme is predominantly pale blue and you have chosen an off-white shade, a complementary pale blue trim will provide a good contrast.

Decorative themes

A more ambitious idea is to coordinate the decorative theme on the shade with a decorative treatment applied to the lampstand. For example, in the American Fireside Crafts Catalogue of 1929, a cactus-shaped stand cut out of a thin sheet of wood is topped by a shade with a bucking bronco painted on it. You could make something similar using a narrow wooden stand onto which you stick paper cut-outs (see pages 56–59). The design could be something as simple as a series of stars, one on top of the other, or alternate stars with crescent moons. If you want the original stand to be hidden from sight when viewed from the front, make sure that the cut-outs you use are wider than the stand itself, so that it is completely hidden. Paint the stand and the back of the images in the same colour; and glue the images onto the stand. Then decorate the lampshade to match the theme – you can paint it or stick on cut-outs.

Zebra Stripes Lampshade

You will need:

> Plain fabric lampshade

> Picture of a zebra

> Pencil

> Small pot of black fabric paint

> Artist's brush, no 6

Method

1 Look through nature books or magazines for a picture of a zebra. Ideally, copy the zebra stripes free-hand. Alternatively, using the pencil, draw a box over one area of the zebra picture.

2 Again using the pencil, copy the section of zebra markings that you have highlighted onto the lampshade so that it makes an attractive pattern.

3 With the artist's brush, paint over your pencil drawing with the black fabric paint. Leave to dry overnight.

Pleated Lampshade

You will need:

- Sheet of thick paper (but thin enough to allow light to shine through), plain, coloured or patterned, such as wrapping paper
- Tape measure
- Wallpaper border (optional)
- String
- Hole punch
- Ribbon
- Paper glue

Method

1 Measure the height and circumference of a lampshade (the same size as the one you want to make) and cut the piece of thick paper to the same height and double the width. If you have chosen plain paper, stick on a wallpaper border for decorative effect.

2 Measure your first paper pleat of 1 cm (3/8 in) with the tape measure. Use this first pleat as a guide for the other pleats. Once you have pleated the whole sheet of paper, score down each

pleat with scissors to make the folds crisp. With all the pleats folded, tie up the paper with string at both ends and in the middle, to ensure the pleats stay in.

3 With the shade still tied up, using the hole punch, make a hole that runs through all the pleats, 4 cm (1½ in) from the top end of the shade.

4 Untie the paper and, on the reverse side, punch holes in the crease of each fold 1 cm (3/8 in) from the top end. (These holes will form a ridge that will rest on the lampstand and keep the lampshade stable.)

5 Thread the ribbon through the lower holes.

6 Shape the paper into a lampshade by holding it around another lampshade; glue the edges together. Tie the ribbon ends into a bow.

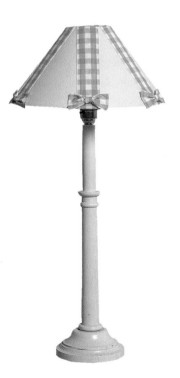

Ribbon Lampshade

You will need:

- Plain fabric lampshade
- Gingham ribbon, 2 cm (3/4 in) and 4 cm (1½ in) wide
- Tape measure
- Scissors
- Fabric glue

Method

1 Measure the height of the lampshade and add 6 cm (2½ in) to allow for turning over the ends and sticking them down. Cut the 4 cm- (1½ in-) wide gingham ribbon into strips. To work out how many strips you need, measure the top circumference of the lampshade and divide by the width of the ribbon. Using

fabric glue, stick the ribbon in straight lines from the top to the bottom of the lampshade, leaving about 3 cm (1¼ in) at both ends, which you turn over and stick down.

2 Cut the 2 cm- (3/4 in-) wide gingham ribbon into strips, tie the strips into bows and stick onto the lampshade.

Plasterwork

Plasterwork in the form of ceiling roses, cornices and mouldings is a marvellous way to add interest to a room. Even a simple cornice helps to define and soften the line where wall meets ceiling, and restoring the curves of a ceiling rose will provide a focal point in an expanse of ceiling. If these features are painted white, they will enhance, not detract, from a scheme.

Many of the motifs that appear in the centrepieces and cornices available today date back to the Romans, who were the first to use decorative stucco work in interiors. They drew widely from nature, mythology and legends for their motifs, which included flower garlands and wreaths and figures of heroes, goddesses and centaurs. These were modelled in low-relief stucco and framed by mouldings such as beading and trellis designs. Most examples only survived where they had been installed in underground rooms and grottoes and were dubbed 'grotesques', suggestive of their location and their often fantastical themes.

Modelled relief-work

Plasterwork from the seventeenth century onwards was widely used throughout Europe, and later in America, not only for features such as centrepieces, cornices and mouldings but also to provide high-relief frames for pictures and mirrors. You can make similar decorative features, using modelling clay instead of plaster and mouldings. Make flowers and leaves into the shape of a wreath to decorate the front of a plain fireplace, or form them into swags or festoons to run across the fireplace and down each side. Doors and cupboard doors can be treated

Right: Classical moulding motifs, such as garlands and wreaths, provide inspiration for your own projects.

in the same way; plasterwork panels of different sizes can be added by ready-made mouldings (see pages 24–27).

Leaves are an easy shape to model as they can be pressed into the clay to form the shape, as shown in the following project. Flowers are too fragile for this process, but fortunately many flower shapes are easy to model. Wild roses, daisies and pansies all have simple yet distinctive outlines. You can find the patterns in an illustrated gardening book or, perhaps surprisingly, from any good cake decorating manual. Rolled flat, icing is much the same as modelling clay, and, rather usefully, cake decorators tend to draw on the same naturalistic forms that are traditional to plasterwork. Pastry cutters are useful for a serrated edge, and you may find some suitable pastry shapes, such as stars, that can be incorporated into your design. If you want to repeat a floral motif several times, make a template out of cardboard and use this to trace round with a knife on the rolled-out clay. For a more realistic look, lightly trace lines in the clay flowers to suggest veining on petals, and use a sharp pencil point to dot in the stamens. Once you have baked the clay and while it is still cooling, gently manipulate the petals to curve up or back slightly to make them look realistic. Once the clay has cooled and hardened, paint the pieces in any colour before glueing. Alternatively, gild everything with gold paint – gilded plasterwork was very popular in the seventeenth and eighteenth centuries. You may also find some ready-made gilded items that you can introduce into the design, perhaps as the central piece in a medallion formed from leaves and flowers.

Clay Modelling on Frames

You will need:
- Plain wooden frame
- Small packet of modelling material (you can buy this at most art and craft shops)
- Leaves
- Sharp kitchen knife
- Small tin of white undercoat paint
- Baking tray
- Glue for sticking clay to wood
- Small tin of eggshell paint (we used yellow)

Method

1 If you are using an old frame, prepare it first by giving it a coat of white undercoat.

2 Roll out the modelling clay to approximately 3 mm (^{1}/8 in) thick.

3 Lay a leaf onto the rolled-out clay and press down, leaving an impression of the leaf and its veins on the clay. Cut around the leaf impression with a sharp kitchen knife (**fig A**).

A

4 Place the cut-out shapes onto a baking tray. Follow the manufacturer's instructions regarding the temperature and the length of time you should bake the clay. We baked our clay for 15–20 minutes at 130°c (275°f). The leaves can be slightly bent when they are cooling in the tray.

B

5 Once the leaf shapes are baked, stick them onto the frame with the glue in a design of your choice (fig B). The clay we used took about 1 hour to harden, so, if necessary, you can reshape a piece at this stage.

6 Once the the leaves are stuck down, paint them in the colour of your choice with eggshell paint (fig C).

C

MORE IDEAS

Use ready-made wooden beading to create a 'stucco work' frieze. Decide on the width of the frieze and then work out how much extra beading you need for each vertical to create evenly-spaced rectangular compartments. Prepare and paint the beading before carefully glue-ing it to the wall. Paint the wall area within the frieze darker or lighter than the beading.

Christmas Decorations

Christmas is the most universally celebrated festival of the Christian year. For thousands of years man brought evergreen foliage or trees into the home around the time of the Winter Solstice as a symbol of life, and by the time of the Roman Birthday of the Unconquered Sun, which was celebrated on 25 December, it was traditional to exchange gifts of green wreaths and candles. Such pagan ways were quickly absorbed into the Christian Christmas, and the custom of decorating the home with greenery and candles has persisted to the present day.

These days to decorate a tree and make it look wonderful is very easy as there is such a wide choice of decorations to choose from. The secret is not to over-do it. A tree that sticks to a particular theme or just a few colours will probably look the prettiest. You could choose tartan as a theme and decorate your tree with tartan ribbon and gold baubles, or you could use just two different colours of ribbon or baubles.

Evergreen branches of yew with holly and ivy wound around florists' wire can be turned into garlands, or, if you do not have the time to make you own garland, and want something that will last much longer, you can buy extremely good looking false garlands. If you add coloured ribbon or gold and silver paper twisted into bow shapes to these, it will look terrific. Attaching garlands to a mantel-piece and placing candles behind them, looks particularly effective. Alternatively, you can hang them over picture

Left: A very warm, inviting and absolutely traditional Christmas scene is created by combining luxuriant greenery with rich red and gold decorations.

frames and along shelves or, if you have a staircase, wind them in and out of the banisters, tying them at intervals with ribbon.

Fir cones are one of the easiest and cheapest forms of decoration and when sprayed with gold and silver paint, they can be used in many different ways. For example, you can hang them on your Christmas tree tied with cotton, or pile them high in a basket with coloured ribbon tied round it.

Children love to make paper decorations, so try making a fat snowman, holly leaves or Christmas trees. Fold over concertina-style either white or coloured paper. Place a cardboard template of the cut-out on top of the paper, draw around the template, leaving the joining edges intact, and then cut out the shape. You will have made a chain of as many cut-out shapes as there are folds in the paper.

Christmas trees are universally known but another older decoration must not be forgotton – mistletoe. This dates back to medieval England and was the main Christmas decoration of that period. It looks best if gathered in a large bunch and tied with a red ribbon with a large bow. You can hang it upside down either from a door way or centre light, so that the old, and popular, custom of kissing under it can continue.

Rose Petal Lampshade

You will need:

➤ Plain fabric lampshade

➤ Preserved rose petals (buy these from a specialist shop)

➤ Household glue

Method

Starting at the bottom of the shade, stick on the rose petals, one by one, overlapping them a little, so that every bit of the lamp-shade is covered.

Three Kings

You will need:

- Three polystyrene balls
- Three plastic bottles
- Scissors
- Gold and silver card
- Paper stars
- Glue
- One square of black felt
- Knife
- Drawing pins
- Coloured paper
- Three squares of coloured felt
- Needle and thread
- Sequins and/or fake jewellery
- Twisted cord

Method

(To make one King)

1 Cut a crown shape out of the card so that it will fit around the polystyrene ball. Decorate it with paper stars.

2 Cut a rectangular shape out of the black felt for the hair and a crescent moon shape for the mouth.

3 Using a knife, hollow out the bottom of the polystyrene ball so that the neck of the bottle will fit snugly into it.

4 Stick two drawing pins into the polystyrene ball for the eyes. Stick on the hair and place the crown on top.

5 Cut a cone shape out of the card to fit around the bottle. Glue the edges of the cone together so that the plastic bottle is completely hidden. Decorate the cone with sequins.

6 Stick on a square of coloured paper at the top of the cone. The corners of the coloured paper should overlap. Tack along the edge of the coloured square of felt and then gather it to make the cloak. Tie this around the top of the cone. Decorate it with sequins or jewellery. Tie the cord around the robe with a reef knot so that the ends hang down at the front.

7 Cut the collar out of the coloured felt and stick it around the bottle top. Then place the hollowed-out polystyrene ball onto the figure.

Lavender Pot

You will need:

- Lavender (you can buy this from a shop selling pot pourri)
- Terracotta pot
- Household glue

Method

Cover the pot in glue. Sprinkle the lavender onto a tray and roll the pot in the lavender.

Silhouettes

Silhouettes have captivated and intrigued people ever since prehistoric man daubed the walls of caves with the outlines of sacred animals. That these powerful images are instantly recognizable to us thousands of years later is proof both of the skill of those early artists and the wonderful immediacy of profile art. Civilization after civilization reinterpreted the silhouette – notably the Egyptians, Etruscans and Greeks – but it was only in the eighteenth and nineteenth centuries that shades (as they were then known) flourished as a popular form of portraiture. Before the photograph, the silhouette was the only easy and accessible method of achieving likenesses by amateur and professional artists, and provided inexpensive decorations.

If you like elegant images from the past and cannot afford originals, you can always copy old silhouettes to hang on your walls. Creating silhouettes of your own family and friends, however, is much more entertaining and personal. Seat your subject in front a bright light and trace the shadow onto a white sheet of paper pinned to a board placed in the correct position. You can leave the profile full size or reduce it down, and then paint it in with black paint. In nineteenth-century America, two very popular silhouette methods were to cut the image out in black paper or to cut out an image and place the hollowed-out piece of paper against a background. The basic outline was achieved as already described, although some silhouette artists were so skilled with a pair of scissors that they could snip out an accurate likeness free-hand in as little as three minutes. Hollow-cut silhouettes look very pretty placed on a wallpaper or fabric background – try silk, satin or velvet, which are all authentic for the eighteenth and nineteenth centuries. And there is no need to limit yourself to stark black. Most artists painted silhouetttes in black, but you could try painting clothes in full colour leaving just the face black.

Personalized silhouettes

Apart from bust and full-length vignettes, conversation pieces depicting family and friends engaged in various leisure activities were also fashionable in the nineteenth century. Some of the most charming examples are of children either at play or posing with a favourite pet. These were painted or cut free-hand, but it would not be too difficult to achieve something similar today using the photograph and photocopier method described in the following project. Silhouettes work particularly well for fairy-tale

Right: A silhouette makes more of an impact if it is hung in a group rather than as a singleton.

characters and scenes; these are a suitable theme for a nursery wall, especially if they are made in bright colours.

Finally, here are a few tips about hanging silhouettes. You should avoid hanging just one in splendid isolation, unless it is large enough. Hanging a pair together – for example, on either side of a wall or painting – looks much better. A grouping makes even more of an impact. It is best to try out various arrangements on the floor first before committing hammer to nail. Sometimes it helps to choose an overall basic shape as a guideline, such as a square, circle or triangle. Check that everything balances well together and that the group is right for the wall space you want to fill.

You can place several silhouettes in a single frame, as shown above.

Making a Single Silhouette

You will need:
- Camera
- White background, such as a white board or a sheet
- Access to a photocopier
- Scissors
- Black marker
- Sheet of white paper
- Paper glue
- Picture frame

Method

1 Take a photograph of your subject's profile against a solid white background.

2 Photocopy the developed image at an enlarged size on good quality paper. (Normal photocopying paper will bubble up when stuck to a background.)

3 Carefully, with a pair of fine scissors, cut out your silhouette **(fig A)**.

A

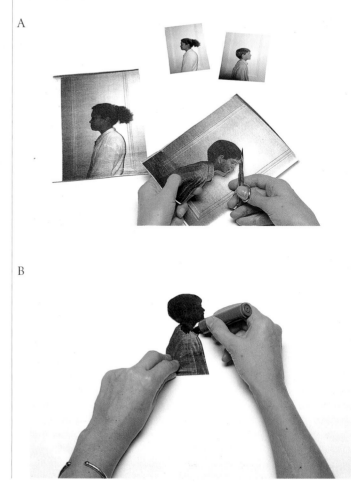

B

4 With a black marker, colour over the image so that it is solid black **(fig B)**.

5 Glue the silhouette onto a sheet of good quality white paper **(fig C)**.

6 Place in a frame of your choice.

C

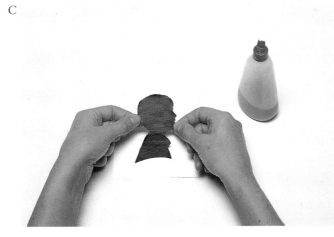

MORE IDEAS

Silhouettes look pretty hung in a vertical line. You can link them by hanging a length of ribbon behind. Finish with a neatly tied bow at the top.

Lacquerwork

The imitation of oriental lacquerwork has a long and rich tradition in the West. It is still popular today, and is used as a decorative technique for giving furniture a face-lift. A number of styles were used in the past, many of them highly colourful, but the simplest for the amateur to imitate is gold-and-black lacquerwork. In this method, a design is applied in gold paint to a black background. The piece is then given several coats of varnish to produce a very glossy finish.

The first examples of this type of lacquerwork reached Europe from Japan in the sixteenth century. The delicate gold brushwork and glossy backgrounds made a tremendous impact. It was not long before European craftsmen were producing similar goods in order to meet the huge demand. Its popularity was so great that, in the seventeenth, eighteenth and nineteenth centuries, 'japanning' and 'japan work' became the generic terms to describe the many kinds of European lacquerwork that were inspired by the Orient.

From the eighteenth century onwards, European and American craftsmen created elaborate scenes on their lacquered goods. These designs, known as *chinoiserie*, could consist of a whole miniature landscape of rugged rocks and weeping willows with boats serenely sailing past a pagoda, or elegantly parasolled figures strolling in a garden complete with fretted bridge. Much of their charm lies in the fact that they only very loosely resemble the originals. Although black backgrounds were common, the English, in particular, experimented with red or coral backgrounds, as well as deep green, blue and yellow. In the seventeenth century, a technique known as *lacca povera*, or 'poor man's lacquer', was used by the Venetians to create coloured

Right: The striking gold-and-red lacquerwork combined with an oriental motif gives this bathroom a distinctly Eastern atmosphere.

lacquerwork. This method used découpage, or paper cut-outs, (see pages 56–59).

Lacquering furniture

The appeal of black-and-gold lacquerwork is that you can make the decoration as simple or as elaborate as you like. A very simple first project is to lacquer a plain wooden chair. First of all, paint it black, then add small details in gold, such as a few simple leafy bamboo stems – a popular oriental motif. Apply these to the back and front of the backrest and to complete the transformation, cover the whole chair with several coats of gloss varnish. Ideally, the decorative brushwork should be applied free-hand to give it the spontaneity of the earlier pieces. If you are nervous about painting free-hand, you can always practice on paper first. You can also trace suitable motifs onto the black ground first if you do not feel confident enough to work without a basic outline to follow (pencil tracings show up well enough on black eggshell). Almost any item can be decorated in this way – table tops, cupboard doors, boxes, trunks or chests of drawers, and smaller items such as wooden lamp bases and picture frames. In the following project, a plain tray is transformed by a simple use of gold-and-black lacquerwork.

Black-and-Gold Tray

You will need:
- Wooden tray
- Small tin of grey undercoat
- Small tin of black eggshell paint
- Paintbrush
- Design or illustration, preferably oriental, to copy
- Chinagraph pencil
- Artist's brush, no 1
- Gold paint
- Wire wool
- Gloss varnish

Method

1 If you do not want to buy a new tray, paint an old tray black. First paint it with a grey undercoat. Allow 6 hours to dry and paint over with the black eggshell paint. Again, allow 6 hours to dry.

2 Draw the design on the tray with a chinagraph pencil. You can either make up your own or copy one from a book or magazine. If you are feeling confident, you can attempt a whole scene such as the one in this example (fig A), or you could do something simple, such as a floral design.

3 Carefully paint over the pencil drawing with gold paint, using artist's brush no 1 (fig B).

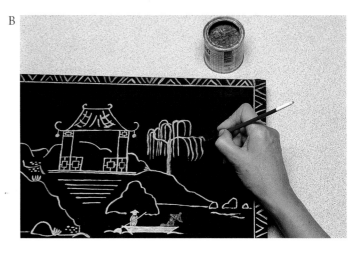

4 Allow the gold paint to dry overnight. Once dry, rub over it gently with wire wool. This will produce an 'antique' effect (**fig C**).

5 Apply at least four coats of varnish. Allow each coat 3 to 4 hours to dry. In proper Japanese lacquerwork, up to twelve coats of varnish would be applied.

C

MORE IDEAS

An exotic background for lacquerwork is imitation tortoiseshell. This can be achieved by using a reddish-brown background with black markings and silver or gold decoration.

❖

Studs

Metal studs have been used for centuries both to decorate furniture and to hold fabric coverings in position. In the Middle Ages, tables and benches were sometimes covered with leather held in place with studs. By the seventeenth century, when upholstered furniture was commonplace, studs were not only used to hold the fabric in position, but were arranged to echo the beautiful shape of the chairs. Eighteenth-century chairs sometimes included a simple scalloped pattern marked out in studs around the edge of the seat, but by the nineteenth century, studs had generally been replaced by elaborate trimmings that hid the upholstery nailwork. Nowadays, studs are used for decorative purposes on upholstery, whether antique reproduction or modern, but the place you are most likely to find them is on leather jackets!

Working with studs

Studs of various shapes and in various metal finishes are available from most department stores and specialist upholstery suppliers. They can be used to decorate upholstered chairs and wooden furniture as an alternative to braiding. A plain wide wooden picture or mirror frame looks good with a straight or patterned border of studs. You could even try the medieval idea of covering a small table or stool with leather and using studs to hold it in place and as decoration. If the leather is fine enough, cut a patterned border to hang over the edge of the furniture, below the line of studs. You will probably need to glue the leather down first, then mark with a pencil where you want the studs to go. Use a small hammer to tap the studs into position.

Right: Studs can be used as an alternative to a braid border on wallpaper or as part of the wallpaper design.

If you remove the pins from upholstery studs, they can be used in a number of other decorative ways. Remove the pins with great care; they should snap off easily if you use a pair of small pliers. Wear padded gloves to protect your fingers. Try sticking studs around the braided rim of a lampshade or, alternatively, if you have braided your wallpaper, you can stick studs on at approximately 5-cm (2-in) intervals along the braid. You can also stick studs onto cushion covers to create an unusual border. Or you can use them to decorate smaller items such as tinware and wooden or metal boxes.

Studding a Cigar Box

You will need:

- ➤ Wooden cigar box
- ➤ Small tin of grey emulsion paint
- ➤ Black marker
- ➤ Small tin of green eggshell paint
- ➤ 2.5 cm (1 in) paintbrush
- ➤ Selection of studs
- ➤ Metal glue

Method

1 Undercoat the cigar box with grey emulsion paint. Leave to dry for 6 hours. When dry, paint over with the green eggshell paint (**fig A**). Leave to dry overnight.

2 Using the black marker, draw a design for your studs on the box (**fig B**). In this example, we have chosen to arrange the studs in the shape of a person's initials.

3 Once you are happy with your design, stick the studs in place (**fig C**). Leave the glue to dry overnight.

B

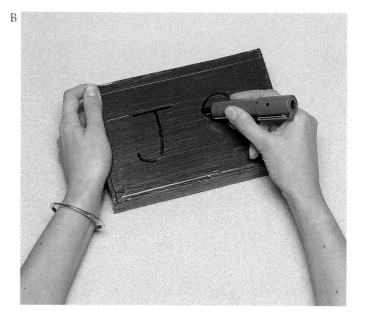

A

C

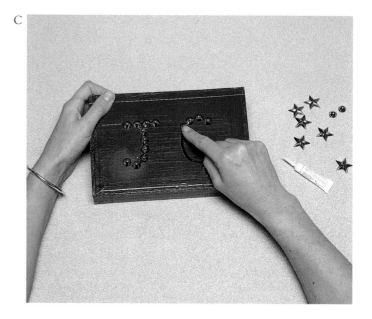

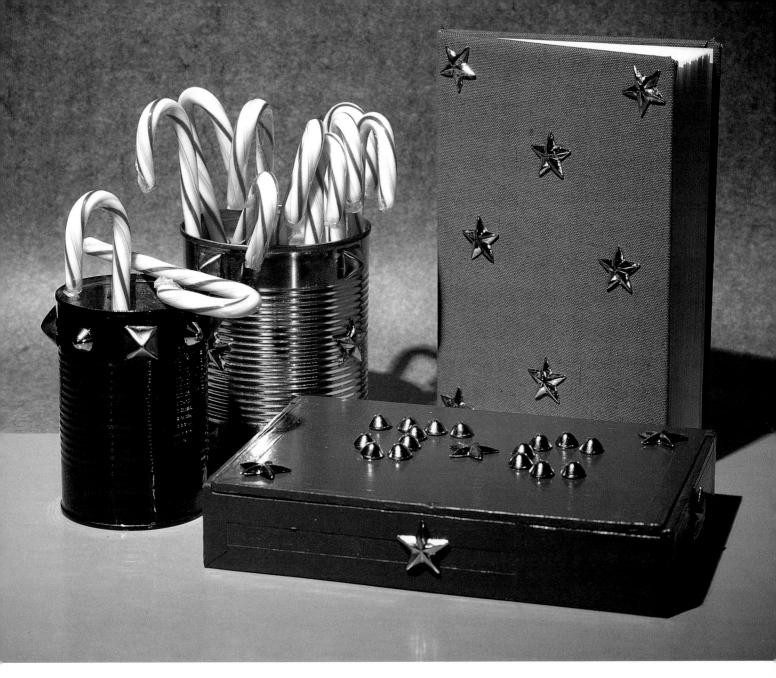

Studding a Diary

You will need:
- Fabric of your choice
- Scissors
- Fabric glue
- Metal glue
- Selection of studs

Method

1 Open the book and place it on top of the fabric. Cut around the book, leaving a 2.5 cm (1 in) border around the edge. Cut a diagonal line across each corner of the fabric border 2.5 cm (1 in) long, making four flaps. Pick up the book and fabric and turn them over. Make two cuts on either side of the spine, 2.5 cm (1 in) deep. Fold over and stick down the two side flaps and then the four top and bottom flaps. Cut the spine flap into a triangle and tuck it into the spine with a dab of glue. You must stick down the flaps when the book is open, otherwise the material will not be spread taut over the book.

2 Stick on the studs with the metal glue. If you want, you can draw dots with a pen where you want to place the studs.

MORE IDEAS
Revamp an old tin can with studs (see above). Simply remove the label and wash in detergent. Dry the can and stick the studs on in a design of your choice. The finished item makes an excellent pen holder. (Before you begin, make sure the can has no sharp edges.)

Curtain Tie-Backs

Tie-backs and hold-backs may be the last thing on your mind when you are buying fabric for curtains, but they can make a great deal of difference to the finished look. They not only offer a means of drawing back the curtains during the day, but they also allow the curtains to be displayed in different ways. A tight tie-back emphasizes a crisp, tailored curtain. A looser tie-back supports a softer, more draped curtain design, which may include displaying a lining fabric. The positioning of the tie-back or hold-back is another important consideration that will affect the way a curtain hangs. Usually they are placed at a mid-way point along the length of the curtain, but it is also possible to position them higher or lower than this. The best way to decide where you want to put the tie-backs or hold-back is to ask someone to drape the curtains for you at different heights, while you stand back and choose which you prefer.

The classic tie-back design is the rope with tassels. This was widely used when paired curtains became commonplace in the eighteenth century, and was a particularly strong feature of Neo-classical curtain arrangements. There is a wide range of ready-made rope-and-tassel tie-backs available, or you can make your own rope tie-back from wool. To calculate how long the finished tie-back should be, hang the curtain as required and then measure around the curtain at the point you have decided to put the tie-back. Cut several thick strands of wool and then twist or plait it (see pages 130–131). You can use strands of the same colour, strands of subtly different tones, or

Left: Nowadays, you can choose from a vast array of trimmings and tie-backs for curtains and cushions.

colours taken from the fabric colours in the curtain. Make the tassels by taking a handful of wool strands measuring twice the length you want the finished tassel to be. Fold the wool in half, then wrap a short length of wool round the looped end to bind it.

Curved tie- and hold-backs

By the beginning of the nineteenth century, the second classic tie-back – the fabric crescent shape – became just as popular as rope. A curved tie-back is always the best shape for drawing curtains aside – a straight tie-back never hangs properly. This is not particularly difficult to make yourself, although again you can buy a range of ready-made ones and dress them up yourself with bows or rosettes. Or you can use a couple of long scarves as tie-backs instead, which can be tied in a number of ways.

Curtain hold-backs offer a curved or straight 'arm' behind which to drape the curtain, and they come in an enormous range of metal and wood finishes and designs. They can also be combined with a rope tie-back. Very plain round hold-backs are ideal for decorating. They can be painted or covered in fabric or have various shapes stuck onto them made out of very stiff card. The last idea will, however, have a limited life. The card cut-outs can also be painted, découpaged or covered in fabric. Traditional hold-back designs include crescent moons and lion faces. A crescent shape cut out of very stiff card and sprayed gold or silver will look attractive (or model one out of papier mâché – see pages 92–95). If you are fortunate enough to come across a copy of a decorative eighteenth-century engraving of a lion's face, this also looks wonderful stuck onto card and trimmed to follow the shape of the head. You may find something in the library, or look out for print-room embellishments (see pages 8–11). Print-room lions often feature a long chain falling from the mouth, but you can always trim this off, leaving just the first ring (touch this up slightly with a black pen so you cannot see where it has been cut). Use a photocopier to make the image larger or smaller as required. Stick the finished shape centrally onto the hold-back, and varnish if you think the surface needs protecting.

Decorating a Wooden Hold-Back

You will need:

- Wooden hold-back (buy this from a soft-furnishing store)
- Cardboard
- Pencil
- Scissors
- Fabric
- Fabric glue
- Wood glue

Materials

1 Draw and cut out a three-leaf clover from the cardboard.

2 Place the cut-out shape onto the fabric and draw around it, leaving 2.5 cm (1 in) of extra fabric around the clover (**fig A**).

A
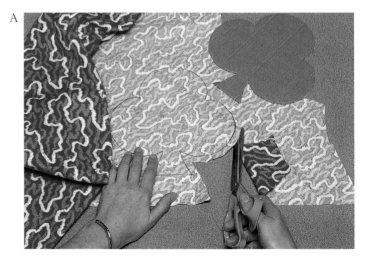

B

C

3 Cut another piece of fabric around the clover. This time it should be exactly the same size as the cut-out.

4 Take the oversized piece of fabric and place the cardbord clover onto the wrong side. Fold over the edges and glue it down (**fig B**).

5 Glue the smaller piece of fabric onto the other side of the cardboard. It will cover the edge of the fabric already glued down.

6 Stick the clover onto the wooden hold-back using the wood glue (**fig C**). Leave to dry overnight.

MORE IDEAS

All sorts of materials can be used to make tie-backs. Lengths of raffia plaited together look marvellous with curtains made of natural fabrics such as linen or calico.

❖

Hanging Curtains

When curtains were first used in the seventeenth century, they were always hung from a rod by rings. Their decorative potential was completely overlooked. They were not hung as a pair at first, but usually consisted of a single length of linen, silk or taffetta, which served to screen out sunlight and no more. It was left to bed-hangings to provide privacy and insulation at night. These were made of the heaviest and richest material that each household could afford, and were lavishly dressed and trimmed. This treatment was eventually extended to curtains, and, by the eighteenth century, pairs of curtains were a familiar sight. These were often festooned or swagged and were finished with a decorated pelmet or valance.

Many of the designs for curtain poles that are familiar to us today derive from the French Empire style, which swept through Europe from the 1790s and continued into the early part of the nineteenth century. The humble rod was transformed into a highly decorative item that was often carved, gilded and finished with finials based on classical motifs such as laurel wreaths and animal heads. These were draped with generous lengths of material in a variety of styles, and often included a second curtain of a lighter material. The Biedermeier period, which flourished in Germany between 1820 and 1860, adopted a much more low-key approach, and curtains were once again simply hung from brass rods. As a variation, fabric was sometimes casually wrapped around the pole and combined with a blind. In nineteenth-century England, Queen Victoria

Left: Blinds and curtains can be combined; here, a Roman blind and swagged heading and tails make a highly decorative feature of a small window.

introduced the fashion for draping a paisley shawl over a pole – a pretty idea for a bedroom today, especially if a pair of light muslin curtains are hung behind the shawl.

Curtain treatments

Today, poles are made from a variety of materials, including wood, brass, steel and iron. They are also available papered, painted and stencilled. Finials range from a plain ball to beautifully carved pieces such as spear and arrow heads, pineapples, artichokes, shells and flowers. When choosing a pole, try and match it to the style of curtain.

Tabs – loops of fabric attached to the top of the curtain – are another way to hang curtains. Again, they can match or contrast with the main fabric. If a tassel or some other decorative device is added at the bottom of each tab, you will achieve a different look. Tabs can also be given a trimming to match the curtain binding.

A slot-heading consists of a fabric sleeve that is ruched up along the pole. Spotted muslin looks pretty treated in this way, although any lightweight material can be used. Sometimes a frill is used above the pole by machining the first seam for the casing a few centimetres down from the top of the folded fabric. With a fixed heading like this, you may need to combine it with a blind. Traditional decorations for a heading include a bow, rosette or Maltese cross placed in the centre, or a series of smaller ones sewn on at intervals.

Although any curtain heading tape can be used for curtains on poles, the easiest curtains to hang are self-lined and have ties that can be attached either to the pole or to rings. You can make the ties from the same fabric or use a contrasting material. Or, instead of making the ties from curtain material, you can use ribbon.

Curtains with Ties

You will need:

- ➤ Enough calico to make one pair of self-lined curtains and ties
- ➤ Scissors
- ➤ Pins
- ➤ Sewing machine

Method

1 Measure your window and allow enough fabric for one and a half times the width of your window. Allow 10 cm (4 in) for the hem and 5 cm (2 in) to fold over at the top. Cut four pieces of calico to the length and width required.

2 Seam up the widths. Put two sides inside out and machine the sides together and then turn inside out and iron. Hem the base of both curtains. You now have two lined curtains, left open at the top edge.

3 To make the ties, cut strips of calico 100 cm (40 in) long, 7.5 cm (3 in) wide. Work out how many you need beforehand. Fold each tie in half widthways and machine as near to the edge as possible **(fig A)**. Then fold the tie with the seam in the middle at the back, and iron flat.

A
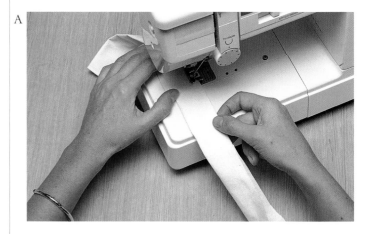

B
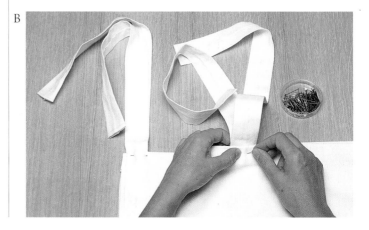

MORE IDEAS

*Instead of making curtain
ties from the same fabric as
the curtain, use a completely
different fabric or ribbon
(see right).*

❖

C

4 Starting at one edge, you will
need to sew in the ties along the
top at 15 cm (6 in) intervals. Fold
each one in half and place between
each curtain and its
lining and pin **(fig B)**.

5 Turning in the raw edges,
machine along the top of the
curtain, sewing the ties in as you do
so. When finished, you can either
knot them or tie them in a bow over
the curtain rail **(fig C)**.

Rope

Rope is a cheap and versatile means of adding interest to everything from walls to cushion covers. Rope has been used for centuries as a decorative device. Rope turnings were used extensively in Elizabethan and Jacobean England on chair and cabinet legs and as a design for wooden and metal candlesticks. The rope design was revived in the nineteenth century, particularly in England and America, when Elizabethan-style furniture was very fashionable.

In soft furnishings, cotton or silky rope trimmings are particularly suitable for cushions and curtains. Running rope across the top of curtain headings, down the sides and along the hems gives a marvellous finish, and if you cannot find exactly the right shade in rope, you can always dye it yourself (see pages 140–143). At the other end of the scale, a really thick piece of rope looks smart running along the top of walls as a simple cornice. Narrower rope made of cotton, hessian or jute can be used to edge walls instead of braiding, and to add emphasis to the top of skirting boards. You can always twist two or three strands of rope together to get the width you want.

Rope works well in combination with shells, perhaps to provide a border to a shell frieze in a bathroom (see pages 88–91). Or you can create a nautical theme in a child's bedroom. To introduce a simple border, paint a wide strip of blue at the required height on the wall and then glue on rope to create an edging. If you leave the rope its natural colour, you will obtain a more authentic look. Stick on paper cut-outs of boats, fish, shells, and so on within the border (if you stick on the cut-outs with a re-usable adhesive, these can then be easily changed). Alternatively, add a series of circular 'portholes' evenly spaced within the border, each one edged in rope. Pick out the portholes in a different colour – perhaps a pale blue or green-blue – and use them to frame suitable paper cut-outs such as fish. Instead of a straight edge at the top of the border, a simple repeating wave motif painted in blue and outlined in rope would emphasize the theme.

Right: Rope is very attractive as a wallpaper border, curtain tie-back and trimming.

Making Multi-Coloured Rope

You will need:

Six strands of wool in each of the three colours

Another pair of hands!

Method

1 Take hold of one end of six strands of wool (all one colour) and ask your assistant to take hold of the other end **(fig A)**. Keep the wool taut. Tie a knot at each end.

2 Each person should twist from their end of the wool **(fig B)**. One person turns clockwise, the other anti-clockwise. Twist very tightly.

3 Fold the rope in half. One person should be holding both knotted ends, the other the looped end.

4 The person holding the looped end lets go. The wool will then twist itself into rope. Repeat steps 1 to 4 with each of the other colours.

5 Take the ropes you have made and repeat steps 1 to 4 to make a thicker, multi-coloured rope **(fig C)**.

MORE IDEAS

Starting at one corner, carefully glue string round a plain, flat picture frame until the surface is completely hidden by string.

❖

Introduce interest to a plain cupboard by sticking on a series of vertical rope stripes. Paint everything the same colour or paint the rope a different colour to emphasize the striped effect.

A variation on the usual rope and tassel tie-back is to have the tassles made of rope as well.

A
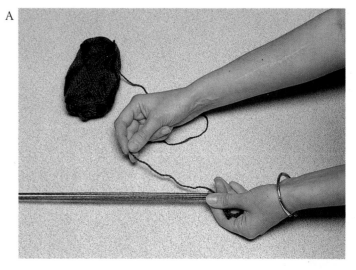

B
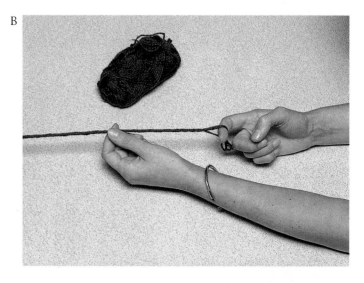

C

Decorating Fabric

Painting and printing on fabric opens up a world of decorative possibilities. You can use special fabric paints to paint free-hand, transfer designs with crayons and inks, or try batik work. Printing with blocks (see pages 48–51) and stencils (see pages 44–47) are particularly easy ways to decorate fabric – the effects are almost magical. Any of these techniques can be used alone or in combinations to decorate a variety of soft furnishings, including curtains, cushions, wall hangings, and bed and table linen.

As an introduction to painting fabric, why not make something for a child? One idea is to to decorate a plain quilt cover with a scene. For example, a long, winding road, snaking its way down the length of the cover complete with stop signs and crossings, is ideal for your child to play on with toy cars, animals and dolls at bedtime. Try out your design first on paper with ordinary paints. Before you start to paint the fabric, stretch it tightly over a padded surface using low-tack masking tape (you should always do this when painting or printing on fabric), then transfer the basic outlines onto the quilt. A soft-leaded pencil – but not too soft – is ideal for this, and will wash out in the first wash. Now start painting! Once you have successfully attempted free-hand painting, you may want to produce a special cushion cover or even a tablecloth.

If you are nervous about copying a very detailed pattern or creating one of your own in free-hand, transfer crayons and inks are a good alternative. They give you considerable control and are very easy to use. Draw or

Left: You can transform plain tablecloths and cushion covers
by painting free-hand or by using the batik method.

trace your design onto paper and then colour it in with the transfer crayons or inks. As soon as the colours are dry, place the paper with the coloured side down on the fabric and press with a medium-hot iron. Test out the colours on a scrap of the main fabric you are using first – they look positively dull on paper but turn into brilliant hues once they have been exposed to heat.

Batik and tie-dyeing

Batik involves a process known as resist dyeing, a quite different technique from any of the above. The design is first drawn in melted wax, which is applied to the fabric with a brush or a tool known as a batik needle (this consists of a handle to which is attached a small metal cup finishing in a slender spout). The prepared fabric is then immersed in a cold dyebath. The wax resists the dye and the pattern is formed.

Batik

You will need:

➤ Plain cotton fabric such as calico

➤ Pencil

➤ Tray, board or frame for stretching fabric

➤ Drawing pins or nails

➤ Batik needle or brush, no 4

➤ Wax (we used wax made from 30% beeswax and 70% paraffin bought from a craft shop)

➤ Double boiler or two pans - one on top of the other – in which to melt the wax

➤ Cold-water dye

➤ Cold-water dye fix

➤ Plastic bowl or bucket

➤ Wooden spoon

Method

1 Using the pencil, draw the design onto the fabric. If you are not confident enough to do this free-hand, draw the shapes onto paper first, then cut them out and draw around them. The design used in this example is a person's initials within a wreath of leaves. If you want to copy this design, you can draw around real leaves.

The fabric may be waxed and dyed a number of times, building up layers of colour in ever more complex designs. The decoration will not reveal its full glory until the final dyeing and all the wax has been removed. The Javanese are the acknowledged masters of batik. The fact that, as far back as the tenth century, the Chinese were offering Javanese batiked cotton cloth as presents to royalty indicates the exceptional quality of the work. If you want to see batik at its very best, the Victoria and Albert Museum in London, the Textile Museum in Washington and the Cooper-Hewitt Museum in New York are just some of the museums that hold fine batik collections.

Batik is really very simple, but you might like to start with a small-scale project such as a cushion cover or a set of napkins, and then work your way up to a tablecloth or a pair of curtains.

2 Stretch the fabric over a tray or wooden frame and nail it down. You should nail or pin the top first and then stretch it vertically and pin the bottom, and then the sides. Make sure it is taut.

3 Place the wax into a double boiler and melt it over the hob. As soon as the wax bubbles, lower the heat. You must be careful as wax is very flammable. You need to make sure it is heated but not boiling.

4 Once the wax is completely melted, you can start the batik process. Dip your brush into the wax, making sure you do not pick up any excess. Carefully paint the wax onto the fabric following your design (fig A).

5 Once the wax is dry (it dries within seconds), unpin the fabric from the frame and crumple it up, so that the wax cracks a little.

6 Immerse the fabric in a cold-water dye bath for the period of time recommended by the dye manufacturer (fig B). You will probably need to leave it in the dye bath for about 1 hour. Dyes vary, so it is important that you read the instructions carefully. With some dyes you will need to use a cold-water dye fix. Check your brand to see if this is necessary. Regularly lift the fabric out of the dye bath; this will prevent dye gathering in its folds. Every 10 minutes or so, stir the water with the wooden spoon.

A

B

C

7 Take the fabric out of the dye bath and hang it up over a bowl to dry. Leave it to dry overnight.

8 When the fabric is completely dry, remove the wax by ironing the design between two sheets of greaseproof paper **(fig C)**. A small residue of wax may remain. To remove this, you must dry clean the fabric.

MORE IDEAS

Sponging with a natural marine sponge gives a wonderfully soft paint effect that is perfect for covers for scatter cushions. Use just one or two colours of paint, putting a little paint of each in separate dishes. Gently dip the sponge in the first colour and randomly dab it all over the cloth. If you are using a second colour, repeat, overlapping areas of the first colour.

Cushions

Cushions are one of the easiest and most inexpensive ways of introducing colour, pattern and texture into a room. In medieval times, when there was little in the way of fixtures and fittings and no one had heard of upholstered furniture, rich householders used piles of horsehair- and down-filled cushions and fabric throws to make even the most ordinary seats comfortable. The average medieval homemaker had to make the most of a very limited range of fabrics. Although cushions were usually plain, they were often brightly coloured and trimmed with a piping, and had a large, fat tassel in each corner in the same colour. For a more luxurious effect, gold tassels were substituted for the plain ones. Sometimes covers were made from two plain colours, with one piece for each side, which was, of course, useful for quick changes.

Today, there is an enormous variety of fabrics and styles to choose from. Cushions can be used to give a specific feel to a room – for example, a few brightly coloured cushions combined with one or two Indian-print throws will instantly give a room an oriental flavour, while the combination of a quilted piece of fabric or patchwork throw and some floral-print cushions will instantly cheer up a room.

It is not difficult to create an impact using fine materials or embroidered pieces for cushion covers. The same can be said of cheaper fabrics, as long as you use a little imagination. Plain cushions benefit from some kind of trim, whether it is tassels, piping or fringing in a complementary or contrasting colour. Introducing a wide border, particularly a patterned one, will also lift a plain fabric like calico. Leave borders straight for a crisp look, scalloped for a gentler edge or gathered into a frill for an even softer effect.

In Ancient Greece and Rome, fabrics for cushions were richly woven or painted, and in medieval times fabric was sometimes painted to imitate more expensive woven items and tapestries. Nowadays, there is an excellent range of fabric paints available; these are easy to use and offer endless decorative variations. This method is especially useful if you want to tie in a cushion cover with a design elsewhere in the room. You can do this by painting free-hand or

Left: You can buy cushions in a wide variety of shapes, sizes and fabrics. They can be used sparingly or, as on this sofa, generously, for a luxurious effect.

by using stencils or printing with blocks (see pages 132–135).

Appliqué and patchwork are traditional crafts that require a sense of design more than skill with a needle, and work well on a small area such as a cushion cover. They are also suitable for large floor cushions for children and teenagers. Patchwork is the technique of sewing together small pieces of fabric. Appliqué involves sewing fabric cut-outs to a larger piece of material. In earlier times, when printed fabric was scarce, needleworkers would cut out the printed images and re-arrange them into a new design which was then sewn onto plain cotton or linen. This gave them more decorated fabric for their money and also used up any material scraps. Any firmly woven fabric such as cotton or cotton blends are good for patchwork or appliqué.

Whatever style of cushion cover you want to make, you will find it useful to start a fabric scrap bag of leftovers from dressmaking and curtains. Fabric remnant boxes in department stores often contain suitable pieces at bargain prices. Most stores also offer inexpensive ready-made cushion pads in a good selection of shapes and sizes.

Appliqué Cushion

You will need:

- ➤ Self-patterned or fine striped fabric for cushion cover
- ➤ Patterned scrap fabric (we used curtain fabric)
- ➤ Scissors
- ➤ Needle and thread
- ➤ Pins

Method:

1 Cut out the shapes you want from the fabric and pin the cut-outs onto the cushion cover. We have used a floral design.

2 Sew on the cut-out with blanket stitch in the following way. Insert the needle into the fabric 6 mm (1/4 in) from the edge with the needle pointing away from the fabric. Hold the thread under the needle point and pull the needle through, forming a loop along the fabric edge. Repeat all round the cut-out.

Painted Cushion with Rope and Tassels

You will need:

- ➤ Neutral cushion cover such as calico
- ➤ Design to copy
- ➤ Pencil
- ➤ Small pot of black fabric paint
- ➤ Artist's brush no 6 or 8
- ➤ Black and white wool

Method:

1 In pencil, draw in your design on the cushion cover. Paint over the drawing with the black fabric paint. Leave to dry overnight.

2 Cut lengths of mixed or plain coloured wool. To make the rope border, follow the method on pages 130–131. To make the tassel, take a 10 cm (4 in) length of wool, fold in it half, and bind the top about 2.5 cm (1 in) from the top. Sew on the rope border and tassels with wool.

Cushion with Ticking Border

You will need:

➤ Fabric for cushion cover (we used ticking)

➤ Scissors

➤ Sewing machine

➤ Needle and thread

1 Cut the fabric to make the cushion cover, allowing an additional 5 cm (2 in) for the border and 1.3 cm (1/2 in) for the seam.

2 Pin the right sides of the front and back covers together and machine 1.3 cm (1/2 in) from the edge. You need to make a hook-and-loop, zipper, or envelope closure on the back cover.

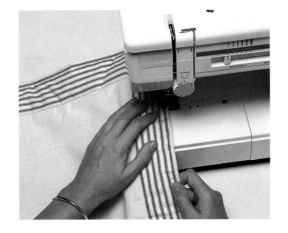

3 Turn the cover right sides out and press. Mark the depth of the border with pins and then topstitch all around the pins.

MORE IDEAS

Lift plain calico cushion covers by sewing on wide borders of embroidered ribbon – either all the way round the cushion or just down two opposite sides.

❖

Inexpensive lace looks pretty made up into cushion covers. Back with plain coloured fabric to set off the lace.

Dyeing Trimmings

Dyeing fabric is such a simple decorative solution that it is often overlooked. Yet what could be easier when faced with a plain white or off-white fabric or trimming than to dye it your chosen colour. Even tired, overfamiliar items are transformed in as little as half an hour.

Ready-made hot and cold dyes for the home market are designed to be as easy to use as possible, and they produce excellent results. They are also cheap and widely available. Yet if you were to go back in time, a tin of dye powder would seem like a miracle. Before the invention of coal-tar based dyes in 1856 by the English chemist William Perkin, dyers had to extract colours from natural sources such as vegetables, bark and fruit. This was a time-consuming and sometimes costly task. In Roman times, the dye that produced the colour known as tyrian purple was extracted from the shellfish *murex* – and the Romans needed thousands of these shellfish to produce just one ounce of dye. Not surprisingly, tyrian purple was designated an imperial colour, only to be worn by the royalty and those holding high office.

Fixing the colour was an even greater challenge to the early dyers. Many natural dyes are not fast unless the fabric has been treated with a chemical, known as a mordant, which enables the fabric to take the dye permanently. Commerical hot and cold dyes do not require a mordant – simply ensure that the fabric is clean and free of any finishes that might interfere with the absorption of the dye. Salt must be added to the dyebath (the amount required is given in the instructions that come with the dye) and commercial cold dyes also need to be fixed after the fabric has been immersed in the dyebath. Cold dye fix can be bought with the dye.

Natural dyes

Although ready-made dyes offer excellent value for money, it can be fun to try natural dyes. There is no doubt that natural dyes, although not always as strong or bright as chemical dyes, produce far more subtle tones. The easiest material to dye with natural dyes is wool or woollen fabric – it retains colour for longer than most other fabrics.

Tea is a classic home-made dye that is fast without a mordant, and has been chosen for the project that follows. You can also use coffee in the same way. Vegetables produce subtle and attractive colours. The outer leaves of cauliflower, finely chopped and boiled for about for fifteen minutes, will produce a gentle pink colour. Onion skins

Right: You can buy trimmings in a variety of colours, materials and sizes. If you are unable to find exactly the right colour, why not try dyeing a bought trimming the colour of your choice.

produce a strong yellow if they are heated in water for about forty minutes, and the leaves and stalks of parsley will give a pretty yellow-green colour if they are chopped finely and heated for twenty minutes. If you use a vegetable dye, you will need to mordant the wool beforehand. Directions for mordanting vary considerably, depending on the recipes you are following, and you will need to consult a specialist book for advice (see Bibliography, page 144). The vegetable dyes mentioned above require a mordant of tartaric acid and alum. Generally, when mordanting wool, you need to simmer the fabric for at least two hours and then rinse thoroughly, starting with very hot water and then gradually using a cooler and cooler rinse. When you place the fabric in the dye-bath, the water should be the same temperature as the last rinse. If you are using vegetable dyes, you need to boil the dye solution. With any type of dye,

you need to turn the fabric from time to time to make sure that it dyes evenly.

Tie-dyeing is a distinctive pattern-making technique using a very simple resist process. Parts of the cloth are knotted or tied with string (the resist), and the whole cloth is then submerged in dye. The resist areas cannot absorb the dye properly, and so patterns are formed. It is a very ancient craft, probably originating in Asia, and it is still practised in some areas of Pakistan, India, Indonesia, Africa and Japan. An interesting variation on the knotting and string resist method is to tie in small pebbles, seeds and beads. This technique is used in India and Africa. Tie-dye is an easy way to decorate bedlinen, towels and and covers for cushions. You can combine tie-dye with fabric paints to create additional decorative touches.

Dying a Fringe with Tea

A

B

C

You will need:
- 1 lt (2 pt) boiling water
- Plastic mixing bowl
- Two tea bags
- Wooden spoon
- Cotton fringe

Method

1 Boil the water and pour it into the mixing bowl. Add the two tea bags and allow to brew for a couple of minutes **(fig A)**.

2 Immerse the fringe in the dye-bath **(fig B)** and stir with the wooden spoon. Leave the fringe in for 10 minutes.

3 Pull the fringe out of the dye bath with the wooden spoon. It will have dyed a very light biscuit colour **(fig C)**. If you leave the fringe in for 1 hour, it will dye a much darker colour.

4 Hang the wet fringe up to dry.

Bibliography

CHRISTMAS

Foley, J. Daniel, *The Christmas Tree*. Chilton Company, Philadelphia and New York 1960.

Kryth, Maymie, *All About Christmas*. Harper and Brothers, New York 1954.

CRAFTS

Margetts, Martina, *Classic Crafts: A Practical Compendium of Traditional Skills*. Conran Octupus Ltd, London 1989.

Wrey, Lady Caroline, *The Complete Book of Curtains and Drapes*. Ebury Press, London 1991.

DECOUPAGE

Harrower, Dorothy, *Découpage: A Limitless World in Decoration*. M. Barrows and Co Inc, New York 1958.

DYES AND DYEING

Green, David and Ashburner, Jenni, *Dyes from the Kitchen*. B.T. Batsford Ltd, London 1979.

Meilach, Dona Z., *Contemporary Batik and Tie-dye: Methods, Inspiration, Dyes*. Allen and Unwin, London 1973.

FLOORING

Lott, Jane, *Floors and Flooring*. Conran Octopus, London 1985.

Clabburn, Pamela, *The National Trust Book of Furnishing Textiles*. Viking, London 1988.

LACQUERWORK

Bourne, John et al, *Lacquer: An International History and Collector's Guide*. The Crowood Press, Marlborough 1984.

MURALS

Seligman, Patricia, *Painting Murals*. Macdonald and Co Ltd, London 1987.

Innes, Jocasta, *Paint Magic: The Home Decorator's Guide to Painted Finishes*. Winward, Leicester 1981.

PAPIER MACHE

Bawden, Juliet, *The Art and Craft of Papier Mâché*. Mitchell Beazley, London 1990.

SHELLS

Critchely, Paula, *The Art of Shellcraft*. Ward Lock Ltd, London 1975.

SILHOUETTES

Hickman, Peggy, *Silhouettes: A Living Art*. David and Charles 1975.

Acknowledgements

The publishers would like to thank the following photographers and organizations for their kind permission to reproduce the following images:

Jo Bangay, page 6; Tim Beddow, pages 88–9; Bery Designs,157 St John's Hill, London SW11 1TQ, pages 28–9; Wendy A Cushing Ltd, Unit M7 Chelsea Garden Market, Chelsea Harbour, London SW10, pages 120–1; The English Stamp Company, Sunnydown, Worth Matravers, Dorset BH19 3JP, pages 48–9; IPC Magazines/Robert Harding Picture Library, pages 25–5, 56–7, 68–9, 80–1, 76–7, 132–3; Maison de Marie Claire/Gilles de Chabaniex/C de Chabaniex/Bastit, pages 40–1 and 91; Galliard/Comte Moireau, pages 116–7; Ianthe Ruthven, pages 84–5; Paul Ryan/International Interiors, pages 96–7; Christian Sarranon, M P Sarranon, pages 60–1, Fritz Von Schulenburg, pages 8–9, 12–3, 20–1, 36–7, 44, 52–3, 104–5, 106, 124–5, 128–9, 136–7.

All other photographs by John Freeman

The authors would like to thank the following for supplying materials:

Prints: Johnny and Louisa Ramsey, 71 Warriner Gardens, London SW11 4XE; Nicola Wingate-Saul, 43 Moreton Street, London SW1 2NY. Fabric on Walls: Nina Campbell, 9 Walton Street, London SW3. Picture Frames: Mel Lappier, 20 High Road, Waterford, Herts, SG14 2PR. Sisal and Lino Flooring: Alastair Till, Sinclair Nelson, 793 Wandsworth Road, London SW8.Tartan: Mike Cobb, Johnstone's Paints, Stonebridge House, Edge Lane, Droylsden, Manchester, M35 6BX. Curtain Accessories and Calico Curtains: Priscilla and John Bradley, Bradleys, The Granary, Flowten Brock, Flowten, Suffolk, IP8 4LJ. Cushions: Valerie Bishop, 39 Carrington Lane, Milford on Sea, Lymington, Hants. Découpage: Belinda Ballantyne, Malmesbury, Wilts, SN16 9AS. Boy's Room: Livvy Stirling, Nursery Window, 83 Walton Street, London SW3. Girl's Room: Victoria Wilson, Young England, 47 Elizabeth Street, London SW1W 9PP. Upholstery: Hugh Garforth-Bliss, Peter Dudgeon, 1A Brompton Place, London SW3. Lampshades: Emma Whiteley, 51 Gloucester Street, London, SW1V 4EY.

The authors would also like to thank the following:

Sophie Fauchier for the use of her house as a location and for the files on pages 16-17; Valerie Bryan, Richelieu, Jim at W. H. Newsons, 61–63 Pimlico Road, London SW1, who supplied paint, wood, paintbrushes and advice. Also Betty Charlton for the use of her kitchen. A special thanks to Helen Dickenson. But the biggest thank you must go to Suzanne Panton, without whom there would be no book.